against

christianity

against

christianity

Peter Leithart

CANON PRESS
MOSCOW, IDAHO

Peter Leithart, *Against Christianity*
© 2003 by Peter Leithart

Published by Canon Press, P.O. Box 8729, Moscow, ID 83843
800-488-2034 / www.canonpress.org
Printed in the United States of America.
Cover design by Paige Atwood.

03 04 05 06 07 08   9 8 7 6 5 4 3 2 1

Library of Congress Cataloging-in-Publication Data

Leithart, Peter J.
  Against Christianity / Peter Leithart.
     p. cm.
  ISBN 1-59128-006-0 (pbk.)
  1. Christianity—Essence, genius, nature. I. Title.
  BT60 .L45 2002
  230—dc21
                                      2002015015

Contents

Preface

I have written an unbalanced book. I have written an unfair book. I have written a fragmented book. I have written an incomplete book. (I think my liver is diseased.)

Had I but world enough and time, *Against Christianity* would have been an exhaustive, comprehensive, thoroughly researched, carefully nuanced and infinitely qualified, multi-volume work. Alas, I have neither.

Or, maybe not "Alas." This book is theological bricolage and lurches at many points toward a form of theological haiku. I have come to think, however, that this is all for the good, for the effect I hope for is the effect of haiku. At its best, haiku glances at the familiar from an awkward angle; it presents what we normally approach straight-on from the side or underneath or inside out and helps us to see it, in a flash, as something wholly new.

I hope that my book has a similar effect. I cannot hope to "convince" readers or "prove" anything here, since I have certainly not provided enough argument or evidence to compel agreement. I hope instead to hint at, gesture toward, trace, or sketch what may be a fresh approach to the (mainly ecclesiological) issues I discuss, more to change readers' angle of vision than persuade.

The *basso continuo* that supports these melodic fragments—that the Church is a culture, a new city, a polity unto herself—is a constant theme in recent theology. New Testament scholars (N. T. Wright, Richard Horsley, James D. G. Dunn, Krister Stendahl), systematicians (John Milbank, George Lindbeck, Oliver O'Donovan), ethicists (John Howard Yoder, Stanley Hauerwas), sociologists of religion (Rodney Stark), historians of early Christianity (Wayne Meeks), and more popular writers (Rodney Clapp, Wes Howard-Brook, Barry Harvey) have all said more or less what I am saying.

Why say it again then?

Well, for starters, I have long wanted to write a book with the word *against* in the title.

More seriously, I hope that *Against Christianity* offers some modest contributions to the discussion. I have attempted to clarify several points and to argue for some under-represented positions. Chapter 1 gives several sizable pieces of exegetical defense for the notion that the Church is a *polis*, since exegetical treatments of the subject are sometimes rather weak. Chapter 3 is about baptism and the Supper, issues mentioned in passing but not, in my reading, given their full due. Finally, after four contrarian chapters, I find something to be *for* in chapter 5, but a cheer for Constantine (not to mention two or three) runs against the grain of recent theology. So, chapter 5 is actually as contrarian as the rest, if not even more so.

Whether these parts of the book advance the discussion or not remains to be seen. A basic premise of the book is that it is far past time that Christians learned to live in refreshed categories, given that the available categories confine, when they do not actually deform, the gospel we are called to preach and live.

*   *   *

Against Christianity began its life as an article in *Christendom Essays*, the 100th edition of the Biblical Horizons newsletter. Thanks to Jim Jordan, the director of Biblical Horizons, for publishing that original article. Jim also read through the entire manuscript and made many suggestions. Jeff Meyers was also kind enough to read through the manuscript and offer his advice. Much of the thinking and reading behind this book was done during my doctoral studies at Cambridge, under the direction of John Milbank, whose writings and conversations were wonderfully stimulating. Thanks, finally, to Doug Jones for his willingness to publish these bits and pieces, and for being kind (or diplomatic) enough to say he liked them.

Peniel Hall
June 2002

1
Against Christianity

1

The Bible never mentions Christianity. It does not preach Christianity, nor does it encourage us to preach Christianity. Paul did not preach Christianity, nor did any of the other apostles. During centuries when the Church was strong and vibrant, she did not preach Christianity either. Christianity, like Judaism and "Yahwism," is an invention of biblical scholars, theologians, and politicians, and one of its chief effects is to keep Christians and the Church in their proper marginal place. The Bible speaks of Christians and of the Church, but Christianity is gnostic, and the Church firmly rejected gnosticism from her earliest days.

2

Christianity is the heresy of heresies, the underlying cause of the weakness, lethargy, sickness, and failure of the modern church.

3

In a sense, I have stated a simple fact: the word "Christianity" does not appear in the Bible, so it is quite impossible for the Bible to encourage us to believe or preach or practice Christianity. In itself, this linguistic fact has little significance. I worship and pray to the triune God, though the word *Trinity* never appears in Scripture. Even the absence of the word *Christianity* is not entirely irrelevant, because it demonstrates that God is perfectly capable of revealing

Himself and His plan without using that word.

More important, however, is the fact that the Bible does not even have the concept of Christianity. This, of course, begs the question of what I mean by "Christianity." On the one hand, Christianity sometimes refers to a set of doctrines or a system of ideas. It is contrasted with the teachings of Judaism, Buddhism, Hinduism, or Islam. By this definition, Christianity is what Christian people believe about God, man, sin, Christ, the world, the future, and so on. The Bible, however, never speaks of such beliefs except as all-embracing, self-committing confessions of God's people. The Bible gives no hint that a Christian "belief system" might be isolated from the life of the Church, subjected to a scientific or logical analysis, and have its truth compared with competing "belief systems."

The Church is not a people united by common ideas, ideas which collectively go under the name "Christianity." When the Bible speaks of a people united by faith it does not simply mean that we have the same beliefs about reality. Though the New Testament does use "faith" to refer to a set of teachings (e.g., 1 Cor. 16:13; 1 Tim. 4:1; 2 Tim. 4:7), "faith" stretches out to include one's entire "stance" in life, a stance that encompasses beliefs about the world but also unarticulated or inarticulable attitudes, hopes, and habits of thought, action, or feeling. To be of "one mind" (Phil. 1:27) means to share projects, aspirations, and ventures, not merely to hold to the same collection of doctrines. Besides, the Church is united not only by one *faith* but also by one *baptism* (Eph. 4:4–6), manifests her unity in common participation in one *loaf* (1 Cor. 10:17), and lives together in mutual deference, submission, and love.

The Bible, in short, is not an ideological tract and does not teach an ideology. Scripture does present a certain view of the world that has true propositional content. But it is an error, and a fatal one, to suggest that, once we have systematized the propositional content of Scripture, the result is a "worldview" called Christianity to which we can give our assent, and there an end. French usage notwithstanding (*christianisme*), it is a radical distortion to think of Scripture's teaching as an "ism."

On the other hand, "Christianity" is sometimes defined more broadly to embrace not only beliefs of Christian people but also the practices of the Church, her liturgies and ways of living in community. This is more healthy than defining Christianity as a system of ideas, yet even here the concept of Christianity conflicts with what the Bible reveals, insofar as the beliefs and practices of Christianity are seen as "religious" beliefs and practices over against "secular" or "political" or "social" practices, insofar as Christianity is conceived of as a "religious" layer added onto human life.

Scripture does not urge us to embrace "religion" in this sense. The Christian is not a natural man who has become religious. Already before conversion, Paul said, many early Christians were highly religious, devoting themselves earnestly to the worship of idols. Conversion, moreover, did not just involve a change of liturgical habit. According to the New Testament, the Christian participates in a new creation (2 Cor. 5:17) and is a Spiritual person in contrast to the natural person (1 Cor. 2:6–16)—a human who is, as many recent theologians have put it, human in a different way. To be a Christian means to be refashioned in all of one's desires, aims, attitudes, actions, from the shallowest to the deepest.

This is not a matter of giving shape to unshaped human nature. There is no formless, underlying "human stuff" waiting to be molded into a Christian shape. We have no "desires" or "aims" or "thoughts" or "attitudes" *in general*. We always desire certain things rather than others, aim in one direction and not another, think about this or think about that—the stuff is always already formed. For the unbeliever, the problem is not that the stuff is unformed but that it is badly and wrongly formed and has to be reformed and transformed into the form of Christ. If one is a

Christian at all, he or she is (however imperfectly) a Christian from head to toe, inside and out. As the late liturgical scholar Mark Searle put it, everyone has a way of "leaning into life," and the Christian strives to "lean into life," all of life, Christianly. Conversion does not simply install a new "religious" program over the existing operating system. It installs a new operating system.

Christian community, by the same token, is not an extra "religious" layer on social life. The Church is not a club for religious people. The Church is a way of living together before God, a new way of being human *together*. What Jesus and the apostles proclaimed was not a new ideology or a new religion, in our attenuated modern sense. What they proclaimed was salvation, and that meant a new human world, a new social and political reality. They proclaimed that God had established the eschatological order of human life in the midst of history, not perfectly but truly. The Church anticipates the form of the human race as it will be when it comes to maturity; she is the "already" of the new humanity that will be perfected in the "not yet" of the last day. Conversion thus means turning from one way of life, one culture, to another. Conversion is the beginning of a "resocialization," induction into an alternative *paideia*, and "inculturation" into the way of life practiced by the eschatological humanity.

In the New Testament, we do not find an essentially private gospel being applied to the public sphere, as if the public implications of the gospel were a second story built on the private ground floor. The gospel *is* the announcement of the Father's formation, through His Son and the Spirit, of a new city—the city of God.

4

Throughout this book, I use the word *city* to refer both to actual cities, ancient and modern, and to "civilizations" (from *civitas*), ancient and modern.

Modernity refers to the civilization of the West since about 1500. Culturally, modernity is characterized by "value pluralism," which entails the privatization of religious institutions and religious claims. Every individual and every group chooses its own values, and civil society is the arena where those values enter into combat. Politically, modernity is shaped by "liberalism," the political system dedicated to the one proposition that political systems must not be dedicated to one proposition.[1]

Though it has roots in the patristic period, Christianity in its more developed form is the Church's adjustment of the gospel to modernity, and the Church's consequent acceptance of the world's definition of who we are and what we should be up to. Christianity is biblical religion disemboweled and emasculated by (voluntary) intellectualization and/or privatization.

Christianity is not merely a haphazard embrace of the values and practices of the modern world. Worldliness in that sense has plagued the Church since Corinth and will be a temptation to the end of time. Christianity is institutionalized worldliness, worldliness accepted in principle, worldliness not at the margins but at the center, worldliness built into the foundation.

Christianity is worldliness that has become so much our second nature that we call it piety.

5

We have made the Church strange and alien to the world, as if she were of a completely different order than the institutions of common social and political life. Paradoxically, the result of this estrangement has been to reshape the Church into the image of the world.

The Church *is* strange: she is the creation of the Father through Word and Spirit, the community of those who have been united by the Spirit with the Son, and therefore brought into the eternal community of the Trinity. She is a city whose town square is in heaven. She is a city without walls or boundary lines, a polity without sword or shield. Of no other society can *that* be said.

But she is ordinary: the Church is made up of human beings, with features that identify her as a culture among the cultures of the world. God did not enter a world of books with blurks; He did not intervene in a world of rituals and meals with spatuals and gleals; He did not call His people to live according to specific quormal principles or to promote a particular uphos.

Rather, God created a world of stories, symbols, rituals, and community rules. Into this world of stories, God introduced a rival story; into a world of books, God came with His own library; in a world of symbols and rituals and sacrificial meals, the Church was organized by a ritual bath and a feast of bread and wine; in the midst of cultures with their own ethos and moral atmosphere, God gathered a community to produce the aroma of Christ in their life together.

Only by insisting on the Church's ordinariness can we simultaneously grasp her strangeness.

6

The Church can cut across the grain of existing human social and cultural life only if she bears some likeness to existing societies. If she is a completely different sort of thing, then societies and nations and empires can go on their merry way ignoring the Church, or, equally deadly, find some murky alleyway to push her into.

But if the Church is God's society among human societies, a heavenly city invading the earthly city, then a territorial conflict is inevitable.

7

YEAR: Sometime in the mid-first century A.D.

SCENE: Conference room, Barnus Marketing Consultants, Jerusalem office.

CHARACTERS: Georgus Barnus, religious marketing consultant; two weather-beaten fishermen named Peter and John; and a spry, sharp-eyed former Pharisee named Paul.

Barnus (consulting a parchment): I understand, gentlemen, that you want to start what we in the business call a "New Religious Movement"—or "nirm" for short. Is that right?

John: I suppose so.

Barnus: I should tell you the market is flooded. There are more religions on offer today than you can imagine. And just because you come from the East doesn't give you any edge. Lots of nirms are coming from Persia and further east, and they're spilling over into Asia and as far as Rome. Maybe you should consider some other line of business. Are you sure you can make it in this market?

Peter: But we have the truth. Those other religions serve false gods, and the living God has commissioned us to take good news to all men.

Barnus: Sure. Well, I'm a consultant, and I wanted to make sure that you knew what you were getting into. Full disclosure and all that; we don't want to end up with some messy lawsuit, do we? Anyway, the first thing we do in this kind of situation is scope out the market, see who the competition is, and find our niche.

Peter: Ah, Mr. Barnus. I need to explain something. You've mentioned the market a few times. But we meet in houses, not in the market.

Barnus (chuckling): No, no. I see the mistake. You've misunderstood me. This is quite funny. I'm using *market* in a metaphorical sense. Imagine there's a market place where people are selling religious things. . . .

John: Like amulets and calves' livers?

Barnus: No, no. Eternal life, satisfaction, contentment, that sort of thing.

John: I see.

Barnus: Very good. Now, I'm suggesting that we think of the various religious options around the Roman world as a "market" in this metaphorical sense. All kinds of religious goods are being offered, there are different methods of "payment," and so on. We need to know where you fit in. What are you offering? Who is offering the same kind of goods? Who's the competition? How do people pay? Is your "price" competitive?

Paul: OK. What can you tell us about this "market"? (*making quotation marks with his fingers*).

Barnus: You said you meet in houses? Maybe the thing to do is position yourself as an alternative to traditional household religions. That would be a tough market to get into, though. Households religion thrive on being dusty and ancient; not many new "household" religions get off the ground. As you know, domestic, ancestral religions are among the oldest and most venerated religions in the Roman world and in Asia. Roman households are all equipped with hearth fires that not only serve as furnaces but as domestic altars. A portion of every meal is tossed into the fire as an offering to the ancestors who are, in some way, identified with the flame. I'm not telling you anything you don't already know.

John: Yes, that might work. After all, Jesus taught us to call one another brothers, and we do think of ourselves as the "household of God."

Peter: That's right. Our worship, Mr. Barnus, includes a meal; we have older men who lead the church and teach us; and we do have women and children in our assemblies. We do want to cultivate the atmosphere of a family.

John: And Jesus said that we had to leave father and mother to cling to Him. He taught us that we are a new family "competing" (*fingering quotation marks*) with old families.

Paul: This is all true. But you are both forgetting something very important.

Peter: What's that?

Paul: We are a household and a family, but we're not connected by blood. You see, Mr. Barnus, we have Jews *and* Gentiles in our gatherings, and people from every land and tribe and tongue. That's part of the good news God wants us to preach. While we may be a household, we're a very unusual sort of household.

Peter (*blushing*): Of course. How could I have forgotten that?

Barnus: Let's list "household religion" as a "subordinate competitor," then. But we still need to figure out your main competition. Would you say that you're a "client cult"?

John: Could you explain that a bit?

Barnus: Certainly. A client cult is a specialty religion, you might say. Each god has a particular capability—say, healing disease—and his priests are able to communicate that benefit to cult members.

Paul: Yes, I know how this works. A person approaches the priest of one cult on Monday for help in his business, and goes to another priest of a completely different god on Wednesday to ensure a safe pregnancy for his wife.

Peter: Well, that's nothing like what we're talking about. It sounds as if client cults don't demand the kind of devotion we expect. That really is like a marketplace.

Barnus: That's right. Client cults have adherents, but nobody "converts" to a client cult.

John: And the gods of those cults are nothing like the God we serve. We're apostles of the Creator of all things, not a "specialty god." He's one God, the only God, and He demands that we worship and serve Him alone.

Barnus: Do you mean that you expect your members to abandon all the other cults?

John: That's right.

Barnus: Well, you might want to reconsider that. That's a pretty steep price to pay. You may not be competitive.

John: We'll take our chances.

Peter: I just had another thought. Client cults don't really form a community, do they? If clients come and go as they please, it's every man for himself.

Barnus: Good point. I can see you're talking about a completely different set-up. Client cults are not really the main competition. What about mystery religions? You know, those cults with secret initiation rituals and all that stuff about dying and rising with the gods. They have a more communal feel to them, and they talk a lot about "salvation" for their worshipers.

Paul: I've never had much time for mystery religions.

John: Neither have I. But we do have a rite of initiation that's all about dying and rising with Jesus. At least that's similar. And I've heard that some of those mystery religions actually wash their initiates, just like in baptism.

Peter: I've heard that too. But, if I understand it right, those baths are not the initiation; they are just preparation for a very complicated initiation. It's not much like baptism at all, really. We just sprinkle a bit of water, and it's over. That *is* the initiation. Remember Pentecost? If we had to put all those converts through a mystery initiation, we'd still be doing it.

Paul: That's true, Peter. Besides, mystery religions are like client cults. Somebody initiated into one of them might be worshiping other gods too. For us, baptism divides between us and the rest of the world.[2]

Barnus: This is fascinating. I brought up those religions first because I figured those would be the closest competitors. But this raises an interesting problem. Those are all private religions. Maybe what you're proposing isn't a private religion at all. Maybe you're talking about a new public religion.

Peter: Like the Jews.

Barnus: Exactly. Jews aren't a client cult or mystery religion. Technically, legally, they form a *politeuma* in many cities, a more or less self-governing community, a "virtual city within the city."[3]

Paul: That's exactly what we're after. We see ourselves as a new city within the city. We're a transformed Israel, a people called to be Jews in a new way. Our groups are like colonies of a heavenly empire right in the middle of earthly cities.

Barnus: Well, Judaism is definitely one of the leading competitors.

John: And don't forget the civic religions. That's what I first thought of when you mentioned "public religion."

Barnus: Hmm. Let me make sure I understand you. As you know, the cities throughout the empire have always been religious as much as civic organizations, and the same is true of the city of Rome, its colonies, the associated *municipiae*, and the military installations throughout the empire. For Greeks and Romans, being a citizen is bound up with participating in feasts and holidays, which include worship of the city's gods. To be Greek or Roman isn't just an ethnic or political fact; it's religious.

Paul: That's still true today, and not just in Rome. Most of the cities in Asia still worship their traditional gods, even if they worship some Roman gods too. I remember being in Ephesus and getting into trouble with the worshipers of Artemis. There was a riot, and I nearly got pulled into pieces. They realized that my preaching about Jesus threatened their whole city.

Barnus: So, you're saying that you intend to enter the market of civic religions?

John: Sure, and don't forget emperor worship. Since Augustus, it has been spread everywhere, and it's bestial. We intend to attack that too.

Barnus: Excuse me? Did you mention the imperial cult?

John: That's right.

Barnus: Do you mean that you're intending to compete with the imperial cult?

Paul: Yes. We're sent to proclaim that there's another king, one Jesus. We preach that there's another empire, the kingdom of God, which brings true peace on earth, not just the truce that Rome forces on people. Resistance to Rome and all its false and idolatrous claims is pretty central to what we're doing.

Barnus: You're talking about another king? Do you understand what this means? The imperial cult is backed up by the power of Rome. I mean, it's not like you could take on Rome and win.

Peter, John, and Paul: Why not?

Barnus: Gentlemen, I'm very sorry. I can't help you. You have completely misunderstood what we're doing here. I don't think you're starting another religion; you're doing something else entirely. I am a religious consultant, not a political revolutionary. I'm afraid that we won't be able to work together.

[*Barnus gathers up his parchments and leaves in some haste, forgetting to close the door behind him. The three apostles shrug, and head off to the temple to preach about Jesus.*]

8

As Bonhoeffer emphasized, given the fact that the Church arose from within Judaism, the Church should seek to be re-formed into a more Hebraic image. This insight, endorsed by many recent theologians, is often linked to a belief that contemporary Jews are still in covenant with God (this view is called "anti-supercessionism"). Though I cannot here enter into a full critique of anti-supercessionism, one point needs to be made: exegetically, it is abundantly clear from the New Testament that the covenant is made with Jesus and with all who are in Him and only with those who are in Him. Anti-supercessionism seems more a result of post-Holocaust guilt than of exegesis.[4]

9

For the New Testament writers, the city of Christians is a heavenly one that will be revealed in the last days (Gal. 4:26; Heb. 12:18–27; Rev. 21). Churches on earth are outposts of that heavenly Jerusalem, anticipations of the final city, joined in a mysterious way, especially in liturgy, with the heavenly city. Every Lord's Day, we, like John, enter into heavenly places, even while we remain in the middle of the earthly assembly. Heaven is in our midst, and we are in the midst of heaven. Responding with homage and worship to the authority of the risen and ascended Lord, the Church is formed as a polity.[5]

Every church is an urban reality; every Christian lives in the suburbs.

10

Though weakened in modern Christian usage, the Greek *koinonia* began its life as a political term. Aristotle's *Politics* begins with the claim that "every state is an association (*koinonia*)," a term that in some translations is rendered as "community." Aristotle recognized that there are various kinds of associations, various ways in which men share projects, goods, and talents with each other. The city (*polis*) is the highest kind of *koinonia*, a political *koinonia*:

> Since we see that every city is some sort of community and that every community gets established with some good in view (for everyone does everything for the sake of what they think good), it is clear that while all communities have some good that they are aiming at, the community that has the control of all and embraces all the others is doing this most of all and is aiming at the most controlling of goods. This community is the city as it is called, the community that is political. (*Politics* 1252a1–6)

Like other communities, the political *koinonia* is establishing on things that are "common" (*koinos*) to the citizens:

> A city is not a matter of sharing a place in common or for the
> purpose of not doing each other wrong and for commerce.
> Rather, while these things must be present yet there is a city
> only when households and families form a community in living
> well for the sake of a complete and self-sufficient existence. . . .[6]
> The end then of the city is living well, but these other things are
> for the sake of the end, and a city is the community of families
> and villages in a complete and self-sufficient life, which, we say,
> is living happily and nobly. (*Politics* 1280b29ff.)

According to the apostles, the Church also forms a *koinonia*
because things are held in common. Ultimately, the *koinonia* of
the Church arises from a common sharing in Christ and His
Spirit (1 Cor. 12:12–13). Christ's body and His Spirit are "public goods," the "common property" of every member. This basic
level of *koinonia* in the Son and Spirit takes various visible forms
in the life of the Church. Having a "share" in the Spirit, each
member is obligated to "share" whatever gifts he receives for the
good of the body (12:7). What the Spirit gives is, as Augustine
would say, only rightly possessed insofar as it is given away. Every gift is a seed, which produces a harvest only if sown.

Table fellowship, likewise, manifests the Church's *koinonia* in
the body of Christ (1 Cor. 10:16–17), and in Acts the members
of the Jerusalem church consider their own property as wealth
to be used for the common good (Acts 2:42, 44; *koinonia, koinos*). For the first Christians in Jerusalem, community life was
shaped by common adherence to the teaching of the apostles,
participation in common prayers, table fellowship, as well as
sharing of alms (Acts 2:42).[7] In several places, Paul urged a mutual sharing of goods, insisting that those who "sow spiritual
things" by teaching and preaching should "reap material things"
from those who benefit, so that there will be "equality" or "mutuality" among all (1 Cor. 9:11; 2 Cor. 8:13–14). Within the
Church Paul attempted to establish an economy of gift-ex-
change, a chiasm of gift, reception, and return gift that repli-
cated the eternal communion of love in the Trinity.

In short: Paul did not attempt to find a place for the Church in the nooks and crannies of the Greco-Roman *polis*. The Church was not an addition, but an alternative to, the *koinonia* of the *polis*.

11

Founded by Philip of Macedon, Philippi became world-famous as the site of the battle in which Antony and Octavian triumphed over Brutus and Cassius. When Octavian later defeated Antony at Actium in 31 B.C., he rebuilt Philippi, established a military base, moved in Roman soldiers, and made it a colony. Philippi was brought under the *jus Italicum*, "the legal quality of Roman territory in Italy—the highest privilege obtainable by a provincial municipality." Since their city had this status, Philippians could purchase property and were exempt from certain taxes.[8]

When he was in the city, Paul got a glimpse of the Philippians' pride in their standing as a Roman colony. Paul and Silas exorcized a girl who was being used as a fortune-teller, and as a result her owners became enraged and brought Paul before the magistrates. Their charges are revealing: Paul and Silas, they said, were "throwing our city into confusion" by encouraging "customs (*ethe*) which it is not lawful for us to accept or to observe, being Romans" (Acts 16:20–21). Paul and Silas's teaching was seen as a threat to Philippi's Roman identity and way of life. As in Thessalonica (Acts 17:1–9), the apostles were seen as subversives, both of the *polis* and the empire.

Philippi's civic pride is important background to Paul's letter to the Philippians. As pointed out by Stanley Stowers, the letter shows marks of being a "letter of friendship."[9] In expressing his friendship with the church, Paul used words related to *koinonia*: the Philippians were partners with him in the gospel (1:5), co-sharers with his trials (1:7), and shared his rejoicing and suffering (2:17–18; 4:14). Indeed, Paul had entered into a *koinonia* with the Philippians by giving and receiving of gifts (4:15), a practice commonly associated with friendship in the ancient world. Similarly, when Paul urged the Philippians to be "of one mind (*mia psyche*)" (1:27; 2:2), he employed language that had been used for centuries as a definition of friendship (Aristotle, *Ethics* 1163b6–7).

According to the tradition Paul invoked in Philippians, friendship was not confined to some private sphere. In the Greco-Roman world friendship was often a quasi-public institution, as much about sharing business or religious enterprises as it was about sharing feelings in private. In keeping with this, both Plato and Zeno the Stoic "understood their communities of friends as alternatives to the social order of the Greek city," and the church historian Eusebius wrote of the Epicureans, "The school of Epicurus resembles a true commonwealth (*politeia*), altogether free of factionalism, sharing one mind and one disposition, of which there were and are and, it appears, will be willing followers." Paul described the Philippian church as a *koinonia* of friends, but that did not mean that he reduced the Church to a private institution. To say that the Church is a community of friends is to say that it is an alternative city.[10]

The political dimensions of friendship come to explicit expression in Philippians 1:27–30, where Paul employed a cluster of friendship terms and phrases: "come and see you/remain absent," "one spirit," "one mind," "striving together." Verses 27–30 are a single sentence in Greek, and the main verb is *politeuo*, which means "to live as a citizen." All these "friendship" terms expound on what it means to "live as a citizen in a manner worthy of the gospel." Philippians 1:27–30 anticipates the language of Philippians 3:20, where Paul declared that the Philippian Christians were citizens of a "heavenly commonwealth (*politeuma*)." The Philippians, so proud of being Roman citizens and so protective of Roman custom, needed to learn to live as citizens of a different commonwealth that placed new demands on its citizens.

These political dimensions are further explored in Philippians 3.[11] As N. T. Wright has pointed out, one of the puzzles of the chapter is the purpose of Paul's description of his own background as a Jew. One aspect of this is clear: Paul presented himself as a concrete example of the attitude he commended in Philippians 2:5–11. Like Jesus, Paul emptied himself of all privilege, and he urged the Philippians to "have this attitude" (v. 15; cf. 2:5). The puzzle is how Paul expected the Philippians to "follow my example" (v. 17), since many of the Philippians were not Jews. How then could they give up Jewish privileges to follow Jesus?

Beginning in chapter 3, Paul conflated Judaism and paganism (as he frequently did). In 3:2, he urged the Philippians to beware of the *katatome*, translated as "false circumcision" in the NASB but actually meaning "mutilation." Verse 3 makes it clear that Paul was talking about Jews: the contrast is between the *katatome* that the Philippians are supposed to avoid and the *peritome* ("circumcision") that belongs to those who "worship in the Spirit of God and glory in Christ Jesus and put no confidence in the flesh" (or in the lack thereof). Though he is talking about Jews, however, Paul described them in a shocking and utterly pagan manner. Since the new age had come, Jews who continued to cut the flesh of the foreskin were no better than the *castrati* who served pagan temples.

Further, as Wright explains, Paul was mounting a polemic against the imperial ideology, affirming that Jesus, not Caesar, is "Lord" and "Savior," both prominent terms in imperial propaganda. Paul's claim that Christians are citizens of a heavenly *politeuma* further indicates that the Philippian Christians are to consider themselves a colony of heaven more than as a colony of Rome. Paul imitated Christ by giving up his privileges as a Hebrew of the Hebrews, and he exhorted the Philippians to follow his example by treating their Roman citizenship and attachment to the Roman emperor as "rubbish" for the sake of Christ and His heavenly *politeuma*.

In short: throughout Philippians, which some identify as one of the least political of Paul's letters,[12] Paul was treating the Church as an alternative to the politico-religious organization of the city and of the empire.

12

We are ill served by translations that render *politeuo* as "conduct yourself." By suppressing the political dimensions of such terms, translators betray themselves: they are thoroughly in the grip of Christianity.

13

The most common term for the Church in the New Testament is *ekklesia*, the word behind the English *church*. Though frequently etymologized as "the called-out ones," the word means "assembly," the "called-together ones," and, like the other terms we have been examining, was originally a political term.

Ekklesia was used in the Septuagint (LXX), the Greek translation of the Old Testament. There, it described the assembly of Israel for covenant-making at Sinai (Deut. 4:10; 9:10; 18:16), for the dedication of the temple (1 Kgs. 8:14, 22, 55, 65), for public repentance, for dedication of the city after the exile (Neh. 5:7, 13; 7:5, 66), and for other religious and national purposes (Judg. 20:2). At times, it refers to a permanent institution of Israelite social and political life (Deut. 23:1). By taking over the LXX usage, the Church was claiming to be the true assembly of Yahweh, the fulfillment of the Sinai assembly, the people who had returned from exile, and the new nation of Israel.

In the Greek world, *ekklesia* referred to the assembly of citizens of the *polis*. When Aristotle spoke of the sovereign "assembly" in Greek democracy, he spoke of the *ekklesia*.[13] When any important business faced the city-state, the citizens would gather in the theater or other public space as the *ekklesia* to deliberate.

In short: the Church presented herself not as another "sect" or cult that existed under the umbrella of the *polis*; she was an alternative governing body for the city and the beginning of a new city.

14

Pagan opponents of the Church have sometimes been more astute sociologists than Christians. Celsus's objections to the Church have been summarized as follows: "Here was a religious association, however extensive by Tertullian's calculations, behaving like a nation, lacking a nation's history and traditions, yet binding its membership to allegiance to traditions and history of its own making."[14]

To be sure, Christians in the patristic age did have some sense of their "national" and "civic" identity, the fact that they were entering the same "market" as the Roman empire, the Greco-Roman city, and other imperial powers of the ancient world. Aristides compared the Church favorably to other nations when he claimed that Christians were "the ones, beyond all nations, who have found the truth," and the rhetoric of Christians as the "third race" was common among writers in the second and third centuries.[15]

Apostolic ecclesiology was not entirely maintained, however. Tertullian was inclined to treat the Church as something like a philosophical club,[16] the Alexandrian theologians treated faith as *gnosis*, a perfected form of philosophy, and not a few monks and hermits in the early centuries heard the gospel as a call to forsake the city for the desert.

Already in the patristic era, Christianity was making its appearance.

15

Ask the average Christian about the relationship between "church" and "salvation," and you are likely to get one of two answers:

either (if the Christian is a rather old-fashioned Roman Catholic) that the Church is the reservoir of salvation, to which one must repair to receive grace; or (if the Christian is a rather common sort of evangelical) that salvation occurs apart from the Church, though it is a help along the way.

Despite the apparent differences between these two views, they are fundamentally similar. Both conceive of "salvation" as a something (almost a substance) that can be stored in a reservoir or infused into sinners directly by God. Both believe that the whole point is the salvation of individuals: for the Catholic, the Church is an essential conduit of grace, but salvation is what happens to the individual; for the evangelical, the Church is a nonessential aid to individual salvation. In both cases, Christianity is looming in the background.

Biblically, however, salvation is not a stuff that one can get, whether through the Church, or through some other means. It is not an ether floating in the air, nor a "thing," nor some kind of "substance." "Salvation" describes fallen creation reconciled to God, restored to its created purpose, and set on a trajectory leading to its eschatological fulfillment. Ultimately, "salvation" will describe the creation as a whole, once it is restored to God and glorified (Rom. 8:18–25). Grammatically, "salvation" is a noun; theologically, it is always adjectival.

Nor is salvation adjectival merely of individuals. If salvation is the re-creation of man through Christ and the Spirit (which it is), then salvation must be restored relationships and communities as much as individuals. If Christ has not restored human community, if society is not "saved" as much as the individual, then Christ has not restored man as he really is. Salvation must take a social form, and the Church is that social form of salvation, the community that already (though imperfectly) has become the human race as God created it to be, the human race that is becoming what God intends it to be.

The Church is neither a reservoir of grace nor an external support for the Christian life. The Church *is* salvation.

16

In our day, physical distances have been compressed by advances in communications and transportation. But have *cultural* distances been compressed? Do we live in a global village?

There is vigorous debate about the answers to those questions. Some deny the existence of a global culture or highlight its limits,[17] while others stress how Western and especially American ways of doing things have affected local cultures throughout the world.[18]

Wherever the sociological truth lies, many believe that a global culture is emerging and that perception is itself an important feature of our world. Even those who embrace global culture, however, recognize that the world does not, as yet, have a "cosmopolis" to provide institutional support for their cosmopolitanism. The absence or weakness of global economic, political, and cultural institutions is a source of concern for globalists. They are not satisfied by global diffusion of musical tastes, clothing styles, films, or the universal desire for jeans and Nikes and baseball caps; they want a global village, with a global mayor and global town council to go with it.

Many Christians are frightened by plans for "one-world" institutional structures, but for all the wrong reasons. The United Nations is *not* a threat because it undermines the sovereignty of the United States. Blue helmets are not important as a challenge to American autonomy any more than the Roman eagle was important because it overthrew the autonomy of the Hellenistic city-states that preceded it. McDonaldization is a problem for Christians, but not primarily because it is gauche (though it is).

Fears like this provide evidence that Christians evaluate the world in terms of Christianity, not in terms of the gospel. If we assume Christianity, globalization is a political (or cultural or economic) rather than a religious concern, and our opposition will be framed in terms of the threat that globalization poses to the current geopolitical (or geo-economic or geo-cultural) realities.

From the viewpoint of the gospel, globalization is a religious *and* political trend, just as the Roman empire was as religious as it was political. Rome was important for the early Christians, however, not because it threatened local cultures but because it was a counterfeit world-empire, which is to say, a counterfeit church. Today, McDonaldization is a challenge to Christians because it involves the spread of Western idolatry of mammon on a global scale. The United Nations is a threat because it is a false church, claiming a false catholicity. Globalists are enemies because they preach a false gospel, an eschatological message of international peace and plenty that will be achieved through liberal political and capitalist economic institutions.

17

If we are preaching the gospel faithfully, we will clash with the various, proliferating religions of the "postmodern" world—with Mormons, Hare Krishna, Moonies, and Scientologists. But, we will also be clashing with other "competitors." The Church's competitors are nation-states and international political bodies like the United Nations. The Church's ethos and culture are not just a challenge to other "religions," but to the ethos of Americanism and the culture of globalization, insofar as such an ethos and culture exist.

But we do not preach the gospel faithfully. We preach Christianity.

And therefore we avoid the clash.

18

According to the standard story, modern liberal political order took shape during the early modern period as a response to the savage wars of religion that shook Europe in the decades following the Reformation. Far-sighted politicians concluded it was dangerous to permit theology to dominate or even enter public life.

Religion is irrational, it was argued, and when religious passion invades politics, the only possible result is bloodshed. Better to organize institutions based on universal reason, institutions that will keep the peace. The best way to do that, it was argued, was to push religious and theological claims and issues far to the edges of public life. Privatizing religion was the price of public peace.

On this point, political conservatism and political liberalism are merely variations within a single outlook. All moderns are liberals. Conservative columnist George Will provides a convenient, and appalling, example. America's founders, Will has argued, "wished to tame and domesticate religious passions of the sort that convulsed Europe. They aimed to do so not by establishing religion, but by establishing a commercial republic— capitalism. They aimed to submerge people's turbulent energies in self-interested pursuit of material comforts." In such a system, as Jefferson argued, "'operations of the mind' are not subject to legal coercion, but . . . 'acts of the body' are. Mere belief, said Jefferson, in one god or 20, neither picks one's pockets nor breaks one's legs." Thus, "by guaranteeing free exercise of religions, they would make religions private and subordinate."[19] If Will is correct about the intentions of the American founding, the American church-state settlement is founded on heretical ecclesiology. It is founded on Christianity.

In fact, this is a highly tendentious myth,[20] but the fact that it is the reigning mythology is of historical significance. Of far greater significance, however, is the fact that the Church has, in the main, accepted this mythology as her own. Christians have agreed that we are a petty and volatile bunch, and that it is better if the Church does not exercise too much public responsibility.

My complaint is not that Christians have retreated from "politics" as defined by modernity, and my solution is not that Christians should get off their duffs and become activists. That would be simply perpetuate Christianity. Christian political activism is as modern and worldly as Christian political quietism, since both are based on the (false and heretical) assumption that being the Church is not *already* political activism. Both assume that to be political we need to do *more* than preach and live the gospel.

My complaint is more fundamental: we have accepted our liberal opponents' account of who we are and no longer see that the gospel is an inherently political announcement, nor that the Church is an inherently political community.

Much to the delight of our enemies, we have embraced Christianity and thereby have become acclimated to liberal order, which we should recognize as a thoroughly hostile environment.

19

Nothing seems more commonsensical to many Christians than Tillich's suggestion that religion is the heart of culture and culture is "religion externalized."Yet this suggests that religion is not *itself* externalized, that religion exists in the heart or the head, either primarily or exclusively, and only at some second stage, if at all, does religion become external. On this thoroughly modern view, religion is essentially individual and private and only by implication or by outworking is it social and public.

Here it can be seen why politicians might embrace Christianity, for if Christianity is an internal religion, confined to the conscience or the heart, then the world of justice, public finance, education, international relations—in short, most of the world in which we live—is *outside* Christianity, and politicians can engage in their public acts without a second thought to what Jesus might have to do with it.

20

Posing the question of "Christianity and culture" makes it appear that we are dealing with two separate things, and that we have to make an effort to show how the two "relate."[21] Framing the question this way ensures that things are getting off on the wrong foot and will likely never get to the right one.

Taking things from the "Christianity" side: if the Bible teaches that true religion exists only as a heavenly city and holy nation (which it does), then what we are dealing with are not two different kinds of things that need to be "related" but with two cultures that are more or less in conflict.

Biblical religion embraces culture.

Taking things from the "culture" side: all cultural effort—building a skyscraper, painting a portrait, erecting a sculpture in the town square—embodies some desire for a better or more beautiful world. Every invention is a wager for utopia. And this vision of the good and the beautiful is ultimately rooted in a religious commitment. Religious factors are not secondary additions to cultural effort; religious factors are always already there, always incarnate in the cultural pursuits themselves.

Culture always embodies religion.

21

David Wells is one of the most prominent recent critics of evangelicalism.[22] Modern social and economic developments—urbanization, industrialization, telecommunications, etc.—have helped to shape a unique consciousness and perspective on life, and this latter is what Wells identifies as "modernity." Wells rejects the deterministic view that social and economic factors *coerce* certain ideas and attitudes, but he argues that social and economic factors exert a shaping influence on consciousness. Modernity, a perspective on life in which biblical religion seems implausible, is the "vortex" created by the swirling forces of modernization.

Many of the evangelical proponents of the "modernity thesis," including Wells, explicitly base their analyses on the sociological work of Peter L. Berger. This is a problem. Sociology of religion of the kind that Berger promotes does not merely posit correlations of social and religious factors—as, for example, the observation that Methodists tend to be middle or lower-middle class while upper classes gravitate to the Episcopal church. Sociology adds to this the belief that the "social" factor has a causative role, and this rests on the prior assumption that "social" and "religious" factors are separable, which is a distinctly modern assumption.

It would be nonsense to ask Moses whether circumcision was a "national" or "religious" rite, since the nation was thoroughly religious in its origins and ethos; it would be nonsensical to ask Aaron whether the penal legislation of the Torah was "religious" or "civil," since it was manifestly both together. Since the gospel is about the restoration of the human race in Christ, the gospel is a social gospel from the very outset. There is not even a moment when it is merely individual and private, for even Jesus appeared within Israel.

Assuming that religious and social factors can be separated, and assuming that religion is essentially a private experience, sociology of religion is part of a secular "policing" of the boundaries of religion. It is one method for keeping the Church and the gospel in her proper—that is, private—place.[23] Berger's theory is a method for ensuring the Church remains within the confines of Christianity.

Wells's assertion that social and religious factors influence each other does not save him from this criticism, for that too is based on the assumption that social and religious factors can be separated and made external to one another at least to the extent that one can "influence" the other. His analysis denies, even if he would not, that social and economic factors are always also religious and ideological factors, that the religious factors are already operative, and conversely that religion is always already social and economic. Contrary to his intentions, Wells's central sociological assumptions are founded on the very system of secular modernity that he sincerely wishes to challenge.

Hoping to make religion acceptable to its cultured despisers, liberalism was an effort to restate Christian faith in updated modern categories. The defense of liberalism was a (twisted) Pauline defense: to the secular modernist, we become as secular modernists, that we might win the secular modernist. To the extent that the analysis of Wells and others uncritically employ Berger's sociology of religion, they are, far from saving evangelicalism from going the way of liberalism, almost exactly repeating liberalism's most serious errors.

They are assuming Christianity, which is to say, assuming worldliness.

22

The notion, popular among "neoconservative" Christians, that the Church is a "mediating institution" that contributes to the construction of a "civil society" between the state and the individual, participates in the same ecclesiological error. The program is well-summarized by George Weigel:

> By being itself, the Church also serves a critical demythologizing function in a democracy. That the church's hope is focused on Christ and his kingdom relativizes all worldly expectation and sovereignties, thus erecting a barrier against the coercive politics of worldly utopianism. . . . [B]y locating the finality of our hope (and thus the object of our highest allegiance) in the time beyond time, the Church helps create the space for a free, vigorous, and civil interplay of a variety of proposals for ordering public life, none of which is invested with ultimate authority. Thus Christian eschatology helps to make democracy and the politics of persuasion possible.[24]

Despite his emphasis on the Church, Weigel operates entirely within the constraints imposed by modern liberalism and secularism. Instead of being an alternative social form, a different sort of city, the Church's political role is to aid and abet the play of democratic debate, to contribute to the pluralistic give and take of civil society. The earthly city's "public life" is the only sort of "public life" that Weigel recognizes; the Church contributes to this public, but is not herself a public. The Church is one sector of a "civil society," rather than a new civil society.

It is no accident that Weigel comes to this political proposal through an eschatology that emphasizes the other-worldliness of our final hope. Though that is true in itself, a failure to see the eschaton realized (by anticipation) here and now in the Church, the failure to grasp the radical alreadiness of the eschaton, permits Weigel to live easily with liberalism and enables him to believe subordination to a larger polity is not an error and a failure for the Church, but the Church's proper public location and calling.[25]

23

The gospel is the announcement that the wall is broken down and therefore the Gentiles are welcomed into the community of the new Israel on the same basis as the Jews; thus the gospel *is* sociology and international relations. The gospel is the announcement that God has organized a new Israel, a new *polis*, the Body of Christ, and that the King has been installed in heaven, at the right hand of the Father; thus the gospel *is* politics. The gospel is about the formation of one body in Christ, a body in which each member uses his gifts for the benefit of all, in which each shares the gains and losses of other members, in which each member is prepared to sacrifice his own for the sake of others; thus the gospel announces the formation of a Christian *economy* in the Church.

The gospel announces a new creation.

The gospel brings nothing less than a new world.

If we are going to stand for *this* gospel, we must stand against Christianity.

2
Against Theology

1

The Bible never mentions theology. It does not preach theology, nor does it encourage us to preach theology. Paul did not preach theology, nor did any of the other apostles. During the centuries when the Church was strong and vibrant, she did not preach theology either. Theology is an invention of biblical scholars, theologians, and politicians, and one of its chief effects is to keep Christians and the Church in their proper marginal place. Theology is gnostic, and the Church firmly rejected gnosticism from her earliest days.

2

There are two problems with theology, one of form and one of content.

Formally, the Bible is not a "theology text" or a "catechism" that arranges doctrines in a systematic order. Paul's epistles have often been treated as mini-textbooks, but they are manifestly not. They are epistles, encyclicals, addressing specific issues in the churches. Paul was not a university theologian calmly writing from a safe haven above the fray. Like the Lord he served, Paul entered the fray. He taught truths about God, but they were taught in the context of conflict and deployed in the form of weaponry. Form cannot be stripped away without changing content, and when Paul's various statements on, say, justification, are removed from the epistolary and ecclesiastical context and organized into a calm and systematic and erudite "doctrine," they become something different from what Paul taught. The Bible is preaching and prophecy, not theology.

With regard to content, theology frequently aims to deal not with the specifics of historical events, but with "timeless truths" of doctrine.[1] But the content of Scripture almost wholly consists of records of historical events, commentary on events in prophecy and epistle, celebration and memorial of events in Psalms, and, occasionally, reflection on the constants of life in the form of Proverbs. Much of the treatment of historical events takes the form of address to the community of Israel, address that includes both invitation and rebuke.

Further, theology is often conceived as a theoretical science, which can, at some secondary moment, be "applied" to practical life. Theology is theory, and the process of "application" serves as a bridge to connect it to the practical lives of Christians and the Church. Heidegger better captured the flavor of Christian teaching when he wrote that "every theological statement and concept addresses itself *in its very content* to the faith-full existence of the individual in the community."[2] When I teach that the persons of the Trinity live in eternal perichoretic unity, I am not merely making an ontological, first-order claim about the nature of reality—though I am doing that. I am not teaching a "timeless truth" that has to be "applied" to the ever shifting realities of an historical community. Rather, I teach about the Trinity as a way of regulating the language and practice of the Church, especially her language and practice in worship.[3] Properly, all teaching *is* application.

3

Consider "theology proper"—the doctrine of God. Does the Bible give us "timeless truths" about God?

In a sense, yes: God is eternally a Trinity, eternally righteous and holy and just and true.

In an important sense, no: we know God as eternally triune because the Father sent the Son who with the Father has poured out the Spirit, and this all happened in history. We know God is righteous and holy and just and true because He has spoken (in time) and because He has acted (in history).

Even theology proper does not deal with purely "timeless" realities.

And how can a "doctrine of the atonement" be formulated as a set of "timeless truths"?

4

Theology is a product of Christianity and aids in its entrenchment. If theology deals with "timeless truths," then all the temporal things we encounter in life are outside the range of theology.

But *everything* we encounter in life is temporal.

Therefore, all life is outside of theology.

All that remains within the realm of theology are (perhaps) ecstatic and "timeless" encounters of the soul with God, God with the soul. Theology keeps Christian teaching at the margins and ensures that other voices, other languages, other words shape the world of temporalities. Politics is left to politicians, economics to economists, sociology to sociologists, history to historians, and philosophy to madmen.

Theology ensures that Christians have nothing to say about nearly everything.

5

Practical theology departments at seminaries do not make theology more practical. They ensure that theology, outside PT departments, will remain impractical—that it will remain theology.

Practical theology ensures that life will remain outside theology.

Practical theology ensures that the secular remains secular.

Practical theology ensures that the Church will remain in the grip of Christianity.

6

Theology is bad enough, but modern theology is theology cultivated into idolatry. Bowing before science, social science, or philosophy, modern theology has adjusted its distinctive language and insight to conform to the common sense of modernity. Metaphysics or evolutionary science or liberal political theory or whatever determines in advance what can be true of God and His ways.

Heidegger again may be cited as a prophet from among the Gentiles. For modern theology, "the deity can come into philosophy only insofar as philosophy, of its own accord and by its own nature, requires and determines that and how the deity enters into it."[4] This is suicide for theologians.

Before it begins to listen to God's word, modern theology has already decided what that word can and cannot say. This is not only suicide. As Barth discerned, it is disobedience.

7

Theology is a specialized, professional language, often employing obscure (Latin and Greek) terms that are never used by anyone but theologians, as if theologians live in and talk about a different world from the one mortals inhabit.

Theology functions sociologically like other professional languages—to keep people out and to help the members of the guild to identify one another.

Whereas the Bible talks about trees and stars, about donkeys and barren women, about kings and queens and carpenters.

8

Theology tells us that God is eternal and unchangeable in His being, wisdom, power, holiness, justice, goodness and truth.

The Bible tells us that God relents because He is God (Joel 2:13–14), that God is "shrewd with the shrewd" (Ps. 18:25–29), that He rejoices over us with shouting (Zeph. 3:14–20), and that He is an eternal whirlwind of triune communion and love.

9

Theology is a "Victorian" enterprise, neoclassically bright and neat and clean, nothing out of place.

Whereas the Bible talks about hair, blood, sweat, entrails, menstruation and genital emissions.

10

Here's an experiment you can do at any theological library. You even have my permission to try this at home.

Step 1: Check the indexes of any theologian you choose for any of the words mentioned in the section 9 above. (Augustine does not count. Augustine's theology is as big as reality, or bigger.)

Step 2: Check the Bible concordance for the same words.

Step 3: Ponder these questions: Do theologians talk about the world the same way the Bible does? Do theologians talk about the same *world* the Bible does?

11

In *City of God*, Augustine discussed the theory of religion developed by the Roman writer Varro, who classified religions as poetic, civic, or natural—the religion of the myths, the religion of the city, and the religion of the philosophers. Augustine's response to Varro was first to deconstruct the distinction between civic and poetic religion. Varro wanted to condemn the latter while justifying the former, but Augustine would have none of it. Civic religion, he knew, was as crass and disgusting as the religion of the myths. Having conflated poetic and civic religions, Augustine dismissed both as insulting to God and the gods, and moved on to discuss natural religion with greater respect and at greater length. In the process, he concluded that some philosophers (Plato especially) came very close to Christian truth.

Augustine's turn from civic and mythic religion to the philosophers was not unprecedented. Most of the earliest post-apostolic writers chose philosophers rather than poets or politicians as their interlocutors, and answered philosophers on philosophical ground. The decision was fateful. A Christian chooses to deal with paganism by dealing with pagan philosophy only if he has made a prior assumption that the Church is somehow analogous to a philosophical school, that is, only if he is already assuming something like the heresy of Christianity.[5]

The *City of God* as a whole, of course, is a vast exercise in civic theology, presenting the *civitas Dei* as the alternative to the *civitas terrena*. Even so, Augustine chose to carry on much of his conversation with paganism in the arena of philosophy rather than in the town square, and that choice has shaped the conversation to this day. It shapes the conversation toward apologetics, rather than prophecy. It reinforces the heresy of Christianity and promotes theology's notion that the Bible is another philosophy text.

It is no doubt of significance that the apostle Paul appeared before kings, magistrates, presumably Caesar, and that he preached in Jewish synagogues, in stadia and in the temple. Only once, to our knowledge, did he preach to philosophers, and that was a distinctly unsuccessful venture (Acts 17). There is a message in that, both about the proper deployment of the Church's energies and about the hopes for success in dealing with the cultured despisers.

12

Mock Chinese Proverb: Choose your interlocutors with care, for some will try to steal the conversation and change the subject.

13

The nineteenth-century biblical scholar William Robertson Smith wrote:

> The antique religions had for the most part no creed; they consisted entirely of institutions and practices. No doubt men will not habitually follow certain practices without attaching a meaning to them; but as a rule we find that while the practice was rigorously fixed, the meaning attached to it was extremely vague, and the same rite was explained by different people in different ways, without any question of orthodoxy or heterodoxy arising in consequence. . . . In all the antique religions, mythology takes the place of dogma, that is, the sacred lore of priests and people, so far as it does not consist of mere rules for the performance of religious acts, assumes the form of stories about the gods; and these stories afford the only explanation that is offered of the precepts of religion and the prescribed rules of ritual.[6]

While Robertson Smith's own account of the relation of myth and ritual has been contested, it can hardly be doubted that myth and ritual constitute the bulk of ancient religions. We need think only of the Pentateuch to see the force of Robertson Smith's observation.

The Greco-Roman city and the Roman Empire were religious as well as political entities, and they were, like every ancient religion, constituted by myths and rituals. There were political theorists in the ancient world, but actual cities and empires were not founded, like Lincoln's America, on a "proposition." Rather, political order was presented, legitimated, and reinforced by myths represented, celebrated, and inculcated through rituals and feasts. We have no idea whether any Athenian watching the Oresteian trilogy went home feeling pity and fear; but we can be reasonably certain that many Athenians went home proud of Athens and her institutions. We do not know whether Plato's *Republic* had any influence on debates within the Athenian *ekklesia* (though Socrates was put on trial for something); but we know that the meetings of the *ekklesia* were initiated with sacrifice and that *ekkesiai* were held immediately after the dramatic contests of the Dionysia.[7] When Athenians looked at the reliefs on the Parthenon that depicted Theseus's triumph over the Amazons, they were doubtless reminded that Athens was the true defender of civilized values, of the proper order of man and woman.[8]

Each religion, and especially each civic religion, also enacted a particular way of life. To be Spartan meant living out of Spartan myths and being shaped by Spartan rituals, but also meant engaging the world as a Spartan. Being Athenian meant learning to "lean into life" in a particular manner. Being Roman was a matter of maintaining dignity and avoiding shame, as well as knowing the Roman myths and performing Roman rituals.

Now—when an apostle showed up at a synagogue in the diaspora, he preached the gospel into a culture, the Jewish culture, that already had its own myths and rites and rules of behavior.[9] When an apostle showed up in a city in the Greek east, he entered a culture that had its own set of civic myths, inculcated from childhood, recited on public occasions, celebrated in the festivals and rituals of civic religion.[10] When an apostle ended up in Rome, he entered a city shaped by myths of Aeneas and Augustus, memorialized in festivals and sacrifices to the genius of the emperor.

And when the apostle came, he came with an alternative myth (which he called the "gospel"), taught his converts to perform rituals of initiation and conviviality (which Christians eventually called "sacraments"), and called men to an alternative way of life (which he called "becoming a disciple of Jesus").

The wandering apostle may have no money in his kit; but he came to town with an alternative culture in his back pocket.

14

It would be nonsense to say this of a particular group of people: "Though they do not wear uniforms, are not organized by rank, do not employ military language, do not enforce rules of military conduct, never perform any military ceremonies, and never engage in military operations—yet in spite of this they *are* the military." (Or, it would be nonsense unless it were describing the French military.) Military culture *is* the sum of all these activities and practices.

Culture is not a shadowy something existing in secret "behind" its "manifestations" in language, rites, and discipline. Culture *is* a people organized and united by its language, rites, rules, and mechanisms of enforcement.

So also is the covenant.

So also is the Church.

15

Let us not talk of theology. Let us talk about the Church's language and myth.

The Church is a distinct "language group." In some obvious senses, this is not true. The Church has a universal message of redemption and it is incumbent upon her to make that gospel understood. Hence, the gospel and the Bible, quite rightly, have been and are being translated into hundreds of languages, and in this sense the Church is not a language group but a multilingual empire. She is inherently and forever Pentecostal.

Pentecost reversed Babel, overcoming the babble which followed God's judgment upon the rebellious nations. At Babel, differences of language bred confusion and divided the nations; at Pentecost, differences of language brought order, conversion, and unity in one body. Babel produced different languages calling on different gods; Pentecost produced the firstfruits of a reunited humanity, every tongue confessing in its own way that Jesus is Lord.

In that Pentecostal sense, the Church speaks and must speak one language. We have one confession, and with the confession comes a distinct way of naming the world and unique categories for interpreting creation and history.

As a language group, the Church is called to maintain and develop her own, Scriptural naming of the world. When the Church enters a new mission field, she always comes into an existing culture in which the world is pre-classified. The Church enters that situation with a new classification and new names. That is the mission: Christian language penetrates an existing language, and the Church begins to attach new labels to everything she finds.

Contextualization be damned. The Church's mission is not to accommodate her language to the existing language, to disguise herself so as to slip in unnoticed and blend in with the existing culture. Her mission is to confront the language of the existing culture with a language of her own.

16

Christianity does not offer a new language, but only some religious words and phrases to add to the stock of the existing language. Christianity offers theology.

17

As N.T. Wright has put it, Jesus called the people of God to be "Israel in a new way," and central to this calling was a new set of names for Israel, or, in many cases, new meaning given to old names.

In His parables and sayings, Jesus challenged existing descriptions of Israel's calling and place in the world. By choosing twelve disciples, He indicated that His followers constituted the true Israel. He said the heirs of the kingdom were more likely to be tax collectors and prostitutes than Pharisees and scribes (Matt. 21:31). With John the Baptist, He insisted that being a blood descendant of Abraham did not ensure God's favor (cf. Matt. 3:8–9) and said explicitly that the Jews who opposed Him were children not of Abraham but of the devil (John 8:37–44).[11]

The whole structure of the Sermon on the Mount is confrontational. Jesus reminded his hearers of what their elders and teachers had told them and then announced, "But I say to you." Jesus gave new meaning to words like "murder" and "adultery," offered new labels to describe those who hate and slander their brothers, and redefined what it meant to be "children of our heavenly Father." True righteousness, according to Jesus' definition, means following the words of Jesus, not the practice of the scribes and Pharisees. At every point, Jesus mounted a frontal attack on the Pharisaical labeling of the world.

The process of challenging old labels and giving new ones continued through the apostolic period. The Old Covenant as a whole was redescribed as a complex of "types and shadows," of which the reality is Christ (Col. 2:16–17). Jerusalem's temple was wonderful, but only a pale shadow of the true, heavenly sanctuary (Heb. 9:1–22). The Jews boasted of circumcision, but Paul said that circumcision by human hands meant nothing and that true circumcision belonged to those who believe in Jesus and who, having the Spirit, are circumcised in heart (Rom. 2:25–29). Paul identified the Church as the seed of Abraham, and said that fleshly Jews were not sons of Zion, but children of the slave woman (Gal. 4:21–31). Paul inserted Jesus into confessions of the oneness of God, reshaping the Jewish *Shema* into a confession of the Trinity (1 Cor. 8:6).[12]

The coming of the new world of the kingdom meant the coming of a new vocabulary, and to be a Christian means to make this vocabulary one's own.

18

For the Saxons, the oak of Thor was "holy," "taboo," and "threatening."

Boniface called it "kindling."

19

And still today, what the world calls "alternative lifestyle" the Church is bound to name "abomination"; what the world calls "pro-choice" the Church must call "murder"; what the world calls the "operations of the market" the Church must sometimes label as oppression of the needy and grinding the faces of the poor.

We should not underestimate the significance of these conflicts over language, thinking they are "merely symbolic." Symbols and especially language (which is a system of signs and symbols) shape the way we respond to reality and help to form how we think and live. Calling a hurricane an "act of God" leads to very different responses than calling it "dumb luck." Speaking of the world as a "gift" means that we greet everything in it with thanksgiving; speaking of it as a "machine" leads some to despair and others to begin snooping around to find the control room. If she is to present herself as an alternative culture, the Church must preserve, develop, and proclaim her own language. Properly, theology is the disciplined study and dissemination of the Christian speaking of reality.

Today, the Church faces a crisis of worldliness. Instead of calling things by their proper biblical names, we adopt the language of the world. When they treat issues of the soul, modern preachers employ the language of psychology, speaking in therapeutic terms and avoiding the severe mercy of words like sin and judgment, wrath and repentance. When they speak of missions, advocates of church growth use language of marketing and consumption, and churches are encouraged to shape the gospel to make it more competitive in a climate in which the entertainment industry sets the cultural pace. Christian political writers claim that when Christians enter the public arena they must adopt theologically neutral language like "natural law" and "human rights" and never, ever utter the name or office of "King Jesus." All these are ways of adopting the language (and culture) of our adversaries, since there is no neutral language.

Blame for this situation lies in the fact that the Church lacks a mastery of her own language. Other languages have filled the vacuum, languages of therapy and marketing, languages of natural law and human rights. It would be bad enough if this failure were accidental, but it is not. Under the spell of Christianity, Christians self-consciously and deliberately adopt and cultivate alien tongues. Christianity insists that biblical language is a special language for Sunday, church, and private devotions, not a language that names the universe and what is beyond the universe, not a language for the market and the town hall.

20

In his 1989 novel, *The Storyteller*,[13] Mario Vargas Llosa, Peruvian novelist and erstwhile presidential candidate, describes the Machiguenga, a scattered and wandering Amazon tribe, whose clans are unified by the activities of the mysterious "*hablador*," or "talker." *Habladores* exercise neither royal nor religious functions, yet are held in high respect by the Machiguenga and carefully protected from Western observation. As he moves from one sub-tribe to another, a *hablador* simply talks, bringing news from other groups within the tribe, and serving, in the words of one of Vargas Llosa's characters, as "the memory of the community."

While celebrating the uniqueness of the tribal cultures of the rain forests, Vargas Llosa is also presenting the Machiguenga as an "Everyculture." Rain forest tribes are not unique in being bound together by common stories. In moral philosophy and ethics, theology and anthropology, "story" has become a central category of cultural analysis.[14]

Stories shape our sense of identity as individuals and communities. For individuals, this is not, as John Milbank points out, merely because we impose narrative structures on our lives after the fact, so as to force some semblance of order on an incoherent mass of detail. Rather, all of us are constantly living out of what Milbank calls "fictions." Alexander was surely an extreme example, but many readers of the *Iliad* have envisioned themselves, at one time or another, as Achilles. Even true stories can function as fictions in this sense, giving us coordinates for our identity, inspiring us to action, and providing guidance for our future directions.[15]

And, the stories that we tell as groups provide a fund of common memories, which shape who we are together by reminding us who we have been together.

Cultures are identified by their stories, and the Church is a culture. It follows that the Church too is defined by her story.

But what is that story?

21

One of the contributions of twentieth-century Catholic *nouvelle theologie*, and of Henri de Lubac and Jean Danielou in particular, was a rehabilitation of patristic and medieval typological exegesis of the Bible. Typological interpretation assumes that events and institutions of the Old Testament present, to use Augustine's terminology, "latent" pictures of Christ. Typological interpretation, in short, sees the whole Bible as gospel, with the gospel narrowly conceived (the story of Jesus) as the culmination of a larger story.

Of equal importance is the insight that the Christ to whom the Old Testament testifies is the *totus Christus*, Head *and* body, Jesus *and* His Church. In this, the fathers and medieval theologians were fully in line with Paul, who wrote that the history of Israel's wanderings in the wilderness were "things written for *our* instruction" (1 Cor. 10:11). The gospel is the story of the Church as well as the story of Jesus. Following the apostolic example, the fathers saw the brides and harlots of Old Testament history as the Church under various guises, and thus they could view Old Testament history as the story of Yahweh's stormy betrothal with His headstrong bride, fulfilled now in the Father's arranged marriage of His Son to the Spirit-prepared Church. Augustine made it a basic interpretive principle that the Psalms are now the words of the Savior, now the words of His people crying for salvation, now, mystically, both together. Psalms is the songbook of the whole Christ: in it Jesus speaks "of us, by us, in us, while we speak in Him."

At its best, then, typological interpretation is quite different from allegory. While Greek allegorists interpreted myths as embodiments of timeless and abstract principles (thus turning the Bible into theology), the fathers plundered the Old Testament to divine the patterns of history. When it has paid attention to the Old Testament at all, modern theology has approached it in a very different manner. Rejecting typology as fanciful and unscientific, many theologians have treated the Old Testament as a purely historical document with little or no religious significance for the Church. Others, no less hostile to typology, see the transition from Old to New as a change from a historical, material, bodily, and social religion to a timeless, spiritual, and individual one (i.e., Christianity).

Opposition to typology not only fuels Christianity but, because of that, assists in the establishment of secular modernity. If the hermeneutical trajectory is from the Old Testament events to the motions of the individual soul, then, as de Lubac argued, Christ's coming has delivered the whole of public life over to the rough play of secular and impersonal forces. So Schleiermacher, the preacher of what Barth called "consciousness theology," says that the Old Testament is to be utterly repudiated as part of the Christian Bible and, consistently, also castigates those who wish to drag religion from the "depths of the heart into the civil world," where, presumably, it can only be contaminated. A privatizing and spiritualizing hermeneutics thus helps outfit a public square that, if not entirely naked, wears a skimpy thing that scarcely covers what looks suspiciously like an iron cage.

By emphasizing that the Church as a real historical institution and communion was prophesied and typified under the old order, typology makes clear that it is of the essence of the Church to occupy public terrain and to occupy it as a public community. And therefore it is of the essence of the Church to deny that the public square is dressed in a flag and nothing but a flag.

If the Church is to recover the gospel, she must recover typological interpretation and learn to repeat, without irony or embarrassment and as a *political* credo, the words of Paul: "Jerusalem above is free; and she is our mother."

22

Typology is often seen as a marginal enterprise—cute, but not the stuff of serious biblical scholarship nor important to the Church's mission. Nothing could be further from the truth.

Typology is one of the chief weapons in the Church's war against Christianity.

Which is to say, typology is one of the chief weapons in the Church's war against secular modernity.

23

Stories define who we are together, and the story of the Church is the gospel, which is the whole story of the Bible, which is the story of the *totus Christus*.

By defining ourselves as "New Testament" Christians, we are attempting to define ourselves by a small fraction of our story. We have institutionalized amnesia; it is a form of insanity.

Is it any wonder we do not know who we are?

24

Contextualization be damned. We have our own story, and if it clashes with the stories we find around us, so much the worse

for the other stories. Our story, after all, is big enough to en-
compass every other.

25

Neither ancient Greece or Rome produced any myth to rival
the universal history found in the Bible, yet Greeks and Romans
had their myths, which were of public significance. Myths not
only embodied a political and religious vision of the city, but
sometimes had direct political consequences. Alexander so identified with Achilles that he set himself the goal of achieving
something of his hero's status, and Martin Nilsson cites incidents
where appeal to myth served as an argument in political dispute:

> In ancient Greece [political mythology] played much the same
> role in the aspirations of the states to territory as the claims to
> nationality play in our own century. The influence of politics
> upon mythology was not small. The great legendary cycles were
> already established, but they could be altered in detail, and it is
> in the mythological padding, the genealogies, that this remodel-
> ing and alteration for political ends is seen most clearly. Athens
> and Megara both laid claim to Salamis and took the Spartans as
> their judge. The latter assigned the island to Athens because the
> Catalogue of Ships in the *Iliad* makes Aias place his ship along-
> side those of the Athenians. Solon is said to have pointed out to
> the judges that the sons of Aias, Philaios and Eurysakes, had ob-
> tained Athenian rights of citizenship, and lived at Brauron and
> Melite. . . . It is significant that the Magarians, in order to refute
> the arguments of the Athenians, afterward declared that Solon
> or Peisistratus had interpolated the said verses into the *Iliad*.[16]

Plato recognized the civic importance of the myths, so much
so that he wanted to exclude the poets from his ideal city because they gave false testimony concerning the gods. Roman
mythology, for its part, centered not so much on the gods and
goddesses of traditional myth but on the origins and destiny of

Rome itself. The Roman empire presented itself as an "imperial polis,"[17] and as such had its imperial mythology.

Decades before Jesus, Rome had already announced that a "Messianic" emperor had introduced a new golden age. Augustus was hailed as a divine figure for saving the Roman Republic from chaos. According to Ovid (*Fasti*, 1.587–616), Augustus "alone has a name kindred to highest Jupiter. 'August' call our fathers what is holy, 'August' are called the temples that are duly consecrated by the hand of the priests. . . . And under the auspices of the gods, and with the same omen as his father, may the heir of so great a surname take upon himself the burden of ruling the world." Horace proclaimed in his *Carmen saeculare* (57–59) that the empire had restored the virtues of ancient Rome: "Now Faith, Peace, Honor, old-fashioned Shame and Valor, which had been neglected, dare to return." Dieter Georgi summarized Horace's poem as follows:

> . . . the *Carmen saeculare* celebrates the miracle which occurred: the salvation of the republic. The impossible had happened. The hope expressed in the *Carmen* is miraculous, no doubt, but present, indeed fulfilled. The confidence about the realization of what had been desperately expected before is concrete, and the materialism of the expectation indicates the degree of reality. There are many eschatological themes: the eschatological language of Urzeit-Endzeit, the ideal of the miraculous return of the golden age and paradise, and even the ideal of the eschatological savior—in line with the heroes of old.[18]

Virgil could likewise write of the Roman empire as the *imperium sine fine*, the empire without end, the last monarchy, the eschatological order of things.

When the Church began to announce its gospel, this gospel of an inaugurated golden age had been in the air for some time. Christians challenged every claim advanced by the imperial eschatology: Augustus, they said, is not the eschatological king;

Jesus is. Rome is not the final empire and order of humanity; the Church is. There is one August king, but he is not the nephew of Julius Caesar; he is the son of God and of Mary.

At the heart of the counter-imperial gospel of Jesus is the story of the cross. Crucifixion was a common punishment for Jewish rebels,[19] a form of execution so horrible that it was never mentioned in polite society. Yet, in the face of this, Paul gloried in the crucified Messiah and saw the crucifixion as a revelation of the character of the "rulers of this world." In 1 Corinthians 2:6–16, he wrote that the "rulers of this age" crucified the "Lord of glory" in ignorance, and this manifested their folly. According to Paul's description in Colossians 2:13–15, through the cross Jesus "stripped, displayed, and triumphed over" rulers and authorities (v. 15). As N. T. Wright points out, this language suggests the actions associated with a crucifixion; empirically, the victim, Jesus, was stripped, made a public display, and triumphed over. In reality, Jesus' crucifixion had exactly the opposite significance: when the Roman soldiers were stripping Jesus, they were in fact being exposed; when the Jews made a public display of their contempt for Jesus, they were in fact being held up for public mockery; when they thought they were triumphing over Jesus, Jesus was in fact triumphing over them.[20]

To exult in a crucified Messiah had radical political implications. Every time Paul said that the criminal on the Roman cross was Lord and Christ, he was implying that the empire was in the grip of some enormity of wickedness and folly. Every time he announced that the crucified Jesus had been vindicated by His Father in the resurrection, he implied that the Roman courts were unjust in the sight of heaven. Every time he proclaimed the story of the crucified God-man, he was posing a direct challenge to the mythology of Rome.

26

The dominant story of America and the modern West is the liberal democratic narrative, which sees history as a struggle between

the forces of enlightenment and tolerance on the one hand and
the forces of ignorance and bigotry on the other. It is a hopeful
story of progress toward liberty, autonomy, diversity, and pluralism. It is a comedy of man's liberation from the irrational traditions that have bound him for centuries.

As Alasdair MacIntyre has argued,[21] liberal democracy claims
to liberate individuals from all tradition, leaving every member
of society free to live according to whatever concept of the good
he finds pleasing, to live out whatever narratives he can conceive. It is of the essence of democracy's story to have no one
story. Richard Rorty is fully in keeping with this viewpoint
when he claims that only madmen have a single purpose in life
(such as seeking the glory of God), which makes Rorty far less
radical than he would like to pretend.[22]

In fact, MacIntyre continues, liberal democracy does have its
own overriding story and its own over-arching purpose. Despite
its claim to liberate from tradition, liberalism is itself a tradition
and has a particular vision of the good society. For liberal order,
the good is to preserve individual choice; liberalism's story of
tolerance and pluralism in practice prevents other stories from
laying claim to the public square. Everyone is free to choose
whatever story or concept of existence that will lend meaning to
his personal life, but the rub comes when you ask, "What if my
concept of existence requires that the whole society be conformed to my concept of existence?"

Clearly, on liberal principles, no one has the right to adopt
that concept of existence.

27

The Church's role in a liberal democratic society will vary. In the
French and Russian Revolutions, "democratic" movements
viewed the Church as an oppressive and counterrevolutionary
force to be resisted and destroyed. Alternatively, democratic society might co-opt the Church's story to its own over-arching

goal. American democracy has followed the second path, turning the gospel into a support for the global spread of democracy and reducing the Church to a timid and tolerant participant in "democratic process." This may not be surprising in itself, since politicians have often seen the Church as a means to a political end. What is disturbing is that the Church has accepted the liberal democratic story as her own, thereby permitting herself to become an appendage to American culture.

This is a product of the heresy of Christianity. It is a product of theology. We adopt the culture's story because we forget that we have an all-embracing story of our own.

28

Much popular Christian history operates in what may be called a "Eusebian" mode, treating America as the culmination of redemptive history.

Eusebius was bishop of Caesarea during the first half of the fourth century, a disciple of Origen, and a suspected Arian who helped to exile Athanasius. In his historical works, Eusebius sought to demonstrate how the gospel of Christ found its crowning fulfillment in the rule of the Christian Roman emperor. For Eusebius, Constantine was the greatest ruler in recorded history and his reign was "the culmination of human history." For Eusebius, contemporary declarations of the "end of history" would have been old news.

William Carroll Bark, in his brief and penetrating book, *The Origins of the Medieval World*, noted that Constantine's conversion filled some Christians with such boundless optimism about the future of Rome that they were "quick to link the welfare of the empire and its steady improvement with the victory of Christianity." The disadvantage of this linkage was not immediately apparent, but once the fortunes of the gospel were tied to Roman political order, the collapse of the latter led to doubts about the sustainability of the former.

Augustine, by contrast, had the advantage of seeing the beginnings of the collapse of the empire firsthand. Remarkably, he also had the wisdom to learn from what he observed. According to Bark, one of Augustine's major achievements was to destroy the

> popular identification of the welfare of Christianity with the welfare of Rome. . . . [H]e cut the tie binding together the fates of the Christian religion and the Roman state. . . . His accomplishment was to prepare the minds of his more thoughtful contemporaries and successors for the possibility of a change in the political state of affairs as they knew it, and to enable them to adapt themselves to this change.[23]

Augustine knew that empires—all empires—are of the earth and are destined to crumble to the dust from which they came. Augustine knew that only the Church is a heavenly *politeuma* and that only the Church is an *imperium sine fine*, because he knew that only the Church has an undying ruler and that only the Church has been ingrafted into the eternal community of the Trinity.

George Bancroft might be excused for hagiographic history, but we, like Augustine, have the dubious advantage of seeing the American system unraveling. The American church does not need another Eusebius to give uncritical adulation to American Constantines. What the Church needs is a renewal of the Augustinian project. We need to disentangle the American story from the Christian story and to insist on the preeminence of the latter.

29

Out of worship are the springs of life. Liturgy is the first form of Christian discipleship training, of *paedeia*, of induction into the culture of the Church.

In the *ekklesia* of the Lord's Day, each member is more and more conformed to Christ, the Church becomes more and more fully the *ekklesia* of God, the body is more and more built up through the Spirit into the full maturity of renewed humanity.

Stirring, that. But is it real? And what does it mean?

30

Worship is history class.

Israel was a people with a shared stock of memories, a people defined by stories about deliverance from Egypt, wandering, conquest, apostasy, exile, and return. To be inducted into Israel involved making these memories one's own and directing one's life by the signposts provided by these stories. Children who did not live through the Passover and Exodus were to be instructed about the significance of the Passover meal and the Lord's demand of the firstborn (Ex. 12–13). Through this instruction and participation in these rites of memory, they were molded into a new generation of Israel.

Throughout the book of Deuteronomy, Moses exhorts the people to remember what the Lord has done for them (5:15; 7:18; 8:2, 18; 9:7, 27; 15:15; 16:3, 12; etc.). For Moses, memory was not nostalgia and often involved more than merely recalling past events. Memory involves memorializing the past works of Yahweh in His presence, and this both called on Yahweh to act again and encouraged Israel for her future tasks. Israelites were to remember what the Lord did to the Egyptians so they would be encouraged to conquer Canaanites. Memory was also to guide Israel in how they were to behave once they settled in the land. Remembering they had been brought out of slavery, they were to treat slaves and sojourners and the poor with generosity and kindness.

Hearing the stories of God's works as they are read from Scripture, listening to the preaching of the Word, singing about

Yahweh's heroics against Philistine and Canaanite, reciting the creeds, and commemorating Christ's victory on the cross at the Lord's table, we, the new Israel, are renewed in the story of God. In worship, the gospel becomes the narrative atmosphere in which we live and move and have our being.[24]

Worship is remembering and celebrating God's savings acts, and therefore worship is history class.

31

Speaking Bible does not come naturally; it is a foreign language. We have to learn to name the world Christianly, and we do this chiefly in worship. Worship is language class.

Preaching is instruction in Christian language. In his stimulating little volume, *Peculiar Speech: Preaching to the Baptized*, William Willimon points out that preaching cultivates "those insights, means of describing, and vocabulary with which Christians describe the world."[25]

But we do not learn foreign languages by listening to someone talk about the language. Teaching is essential, but so is drill, repetition, dry rote. Worship is training in godly habits, habits of speech as well as godly habits of conduct. If biblical language is to become the idiom of the Church's speech, Christians must not only listen to but also say and sing and recite the Scriptures in worship. Many evangelicals object to repetition in worship because they consider it "dry rote." Jesus did, of course, warn against "vain repetition," but repetition itself is unavoidable, and Christian worship needs a great deal *more* dry rote. That is precisely what we need in order to learn a new and alien language.

This perspective underscores the wisdom of the tradition of structured liturgy, with a fixed ordinary of spoken and sung Scripture. Traditional liturgies, with their "boring" and "hidebound" recitation of Psalms, creeds, and rote prayers, drill converts in their new language. Worshipers are made part of the culture of the Church, and, more importantly, that culture is made part of the worshiper.

32

Worship is Political Science 101.

In every worship service, the Christian *ekklesia* is renewed in her unique story and language, her unique political experience and vocation. Every worship service is a challenge to Caesar, because every Lord's Day we bow to a Man on the throne of heaven, to whom even great Caesar must bow. O'Donovan claims that all political order rests on a people's homage to authority, which is to say, on an act of worship.[26] Every Lord's Day, the Church is reconstituted as a polity whose obedience is owed to Christ, and we are taught to name Jesus as King of kings and Lord of lords.

33

Worship is Psychology class.

The Psalms, Calvin said, are a virtual textbook of the human soul, the central text in biblical psychology. As such, the Psalms give expression to all the experiences of the Christian life; they give words to our pains, joys, afflictions, despair, and by giving language to our experience they bring those experiences under description, make them knowable as our Father's loving care for us.

The Psalms are also a textbook of prayer, frequently employing language that is unnerving in its vehemence. Psalms indicate that an overwhelming desire for justice should animate our prayers, that we should express our disappointments with honesty, that prayer is not "quiet time" but a time of wrestling and passion. Contemporary hymnology, by contrast, gives us words for a small segment of our experience, the happy, fluffy, light experiences of life. If we are trained in prayer by contemporary praise choruses, when we face the pains and tests of life, we will lack the vocabulary to name them.[27]

Singing the Psalms makes the biblical story and biblical language part of us, knits it into the fabric of our flesh.

34

Several years ago, I happened to be visiting my parents when a longtime friend of my mother died. As I left the funeral, I spoke briefly to the woman's son and in parting said, "The Lord be with you." Without hesitation, he responded, "And also with you." We had not seen one another in nearly a decade, but in that moment our common training in the Lutheran liturgy gave us words to say—*Christian* words—words of comfort and encouragement in the face of death.

Our common training in liturgy had taught us, in that moment at least, to speak Christianly.

3
Against Sacraments

1

Modernity is a revolt against ritual, and the modern city is an unprecedented attempt to form a civic community without a festive center.

2

Mary Douglas has written that "One of the gravest problems of our day is the lack of commitment to common symbols." This is not merely a matter of "fragmentation into small groups," which, Douglas says, is fairly understandable, but instead "a wide-spread, explicit rejection of rituals as such. Ritual is become a bad word signifying empty conformity." Centuries after the Reformers stripped the altars, "we find ourselves, here and now, reliving a world-wide revolt against ritualism."[1]

Douglas is surely right, but she does not go nearly far enough. It is not simply that we lack "common symbols" and resist "ritualism," but that this is a defining characteristic of modernity.

The reasons for this are many. Among them is the modern celebration of novelty. Sometime in the eighteenth century, according to Ian Watt's *Rise of the Novel*, the meaning of the word *original* shifted. Before, the word had been related to its etymological cousin *origin* and described something that had persisted from the time of the origin; something was "original" if it had been present at the creation. Since the eighteenth century, "original"

means fresh and new, having no relation to the origin or to anything between the origin and the present moment. This semantic
example encapsulates the sea-change in mentality that took
place in the early modern period. Modernity arose as an ideology committed to novelty, to spontaneity, to the now. Ritual,
with its atmosphere of ancient authority and its (apparently)
bland repetitions, was out of step with modern consciousness.
Moderns would rather die than do it over again.

Add to that the fact that common symbols conflict with liberal modernity's cultivation of diversity, and you have a few in-
gredients of the recipe for civilization without ritual.

Much has changed since Douglas wrote her book, partly because of her own influence. Ritual studies has become a growth
industry within cultural anthropology, and ritual has become a
topic across academic disciplines. More popularly, the burgeon-
ing of New Religious Movements, especially those associated
with the New Age Movement, have emphasized ritual aspects of
religion. Still, Douglas's comments hit home. If ritual has seen
something of a rebirth, it has by and large been confined to private and even domestic settings. Witches gather to perform their
rites, but they might as well be gathering for the sewing circle,
so private are their rites. Pagans dress in Druid gowns and form
their sacred circles, but they do it all off in the woods. It is still
the case that we lack publicly agreed symbols and public participation in rituals.

3

Removing the crèche from the town square is the very essence
of modernity, whose first commandment is "Thou shalt have no
common symbols."

4

For modernist romantics, the street was the symbol of the vital-
ity of the city and of modern life in general, but for the urban

planners and architects of the early twentieth century, the street was the enemy. Le Corbusier's battle cry was "We must kill the street."[2] In New York and elsewhere, highways cut through neighborhoods, breaking up decades-old patterns of social intercourse and economic exchange and playing a role in the decay of inner-city America. Housing became vertical, shrouding the street in the shadows of skyscrapers. Parkways replaced streets, and the city became a restless whirl of traffic.

Life on the street had, according to Jane Jacobs, provided the rhythm of urban life, what she called the "rituals" of urban living and which she likened to a "dance," even "an intricate ballet in which the individual dancers and ensembles all have distinctive parts which miraculously reinforce each other and compose an orderly whole."[3] This hardly qualifies as urban festivity, but the life of the street did gave something like order and rhythm to the bustling energy of the city. It gave a human face to modern urban living. At least, the street observed the natural patterns of dawn and dusk. Modernism in architecture and city planning destroyed that. In a modernist city, there is no street, and with the disappearance of the street, the dance comes to an end. In the modernist city, no quarter is given to these rhythms, not even the natural ritual of light and darkness.

As the only alternative to dance is chaos, it is not surprising that the destruction of the dance of the street in the first half of the twentieth century was followed by the urban chaos of the 1960s and early 1970s. Urban planners were not slow in taking the hint and began to see "spectacle" as a means for addressing the disruption of urban life and a way of fostering community spirit to unify the millions living in cities. David Harvey writes of Baltimore:

> [R]iots threatened the vitality of downtown and the viability of investments already made. The leaders sought a symbol around which to build the idea of the city as a community, a city which could believe in itself sufficiently to overcome the divisions and

the siege mentality with which the common citizenry approached downtown and its public spaces. "Spawned by the necessity to arrest the fear and disuse of downtown areas caused
by civic unrest in the late 1960s," said a later Department of
Housing and Urban Development report, "the Baltimore City
Fair was originated . . . as a way to promote urban redevelop-
ment." The fair set out to celebrate the neighbourhood and ethnic diversity in the city, even went out of its way to promote
ethnic (as opposed to racial) identity.[4]

Mike Featherstone has explained the theory behind
postmodern urban spectacle in similar terms. Postmodernism
has "moved beyond individualism with a communal feeling being
generated, to a new 'aesthetic paradigm' in which masses of
people come together in temporary emotional communities."
Though this may simulate community, Featherstone notes that
they are in reality little more than "post-modern tribes" that experience "intense moments of ecstasy, empathy, and affectual
immediacy" rather than genuine, settled community life.[5]

Graham Ward summarizes the postmodern civic myth and
ritual:

> The staging of public spectacle (festivals for this and that, open-
> air concerts in central parks etc.), the exaltation of the kitsch,
> the glorification of the superficial, the enormous investment in
> sports and leisure centres, the new commodification of the
> city's past (manufacturing a nostalgia that substitutes for conti-
> nuity and tradition), the inflationary suggestions of its state-of-
> the-art future, its 'under-construction' technicolour present
> (China towns, heritage centres, gay villages, theme bars etc.)—
> these are the characteristics of the new city-myth.[6]

Whatever may be said about this vision, the artificiality of the
postmodern city perpetuates the modernist revolt against ritual.
Spectacle is no substitute, manufactured spectacle especially. The

postmodern city continues the modernist project—civic life without rituals or unifying festivals.

The result is the anti-city, a mass of people with no communal center or identity.

5

And yet, even Americans, notoriously deaf to symbols and puritanical in our rejection of ritual, identify ourselves by common respect for the American flag, honor to symbolic heroes (Washington, Jefferson, and—for some—Lincoln), celebrations and rituals at holidays, common veneration for sacred sites (most especially, today, Ground Zero).

In spite of it all, we are still programmed as "Americans" by our rituals.

6

Six overlapping tendencies make it difficult for evangelicals to grasp baptism and the Lord's Supper.

First, a spiritualizing reading of redemptive history: "When Jesus removed the special status of Jerusalem as the place where God was to be worshiped (John 4:7–24), he signaled the abolition of all the material forms that constituted the typological Old Testament system."[7] The move from Old to New is thus seen as a move from ritual to non-ritual, from physical to less physical forms of worship. Baptism and the Supper seem anomalous throwbacks to an earlier era: what use do "spiritual" churches have for these rituals?

Second, the prophets: Israel's prophets inveighed against empty formalism, and some conclude from this that the prophets condemned form and ritual as such.

Third, the Reformation: The Reformers taught that the Word has priority over the sacraments. Salvation comes from hearing the Word with faith, not by mechanical adherence to the sacramental system of the Church. Sacraments are an "appendix" to the Word.

Fourth, individualism: The frame of reference for nearly everything, including worship and sacraments, is the individual person and his experience of the world. So, in sacramental theology we ask questions like, "What benefit do I receive from the sacrament?" or "What grace does the individual child receive from baptism?" And we wonder why we need these objects and substances to communicate these benefits.

Fifth, inwardness: Grace is invisible, so why do I need visible substances to receive grace? Moreover, what is really important is my spiritual heart-relationship with God; my outer physical actions are of lesser significance. What matters is the "me" lurking behind the roles I play and the things I do. What happens on the outside never touches that inner self that is unchangeably me. What good then is an external bath, physical food?

Finally, privatization: Religion is a matter of belief and personal devotion. Public rituals can be faked, and so those who tie religion to public rituals tempt us to be hypocrites.

7

In the end, all these factors reduce to one: the Church has embraced modernity's disdain for ritual, though we have given pious glosses to our worldliness.

In the end, all these factors are part and parcel of our adherence to Christianity.

8

Baptism and the Supper as appendixes to the Word: Despite its venerable pedigree, this is not a useful way to approach the issue. We are able to understand the Word without the help of the appendix, as we can read many books with profit without reading the appendix. So long as baptism and the Supper are seen as "appendixes," they will be seen as expendable. Characterizing baptism and the Supper as "appendixes" to the Word, further, is part and parcel of a Protestant tendency toward the "primacy of the intellect." It is rationalism, in that it reduces baptism and the Supper to a means for communicating information. But that is not what rituals are *for*. Treating baptism and the Supper as disguised sermons reduces them so they can be encompassed and tamed by Christianity.

Individualism: As God is one and three, as God's being is being in communion, so human being is being in communion. Made in the image of the triune God, we are always embedded in networks of relationship, long before we are conscious of that fact. Before we could talk or "make up our own mind," we were addressed, talked to, kissed, smiled at. The only "individuals" in the Bible are idols and their worshipers, who have all the equipment for relating to others and the world but cannot make use of it (cf. Ps. 115). Because of our individualistic bias, we cannot recognize that the "sacraments" are rituals of a new society, public festivals of a new civic order. And, individualism is part and parcel of the heresy of Christianity.

Religion and interiority: This has a certain plausibility because Scripture does talk about inner man and outer man, about body and soul. Yet, Scripture makes no hard or absolute demarcation between inner and outer. When people eat and drink, Scripture says their "souls" are refreshed (e.g., 1 Sam. 30:12), and exterior discipline of our children purges foolishness from their hearts (Prov. 22:15). So, outer events invade the inner life. And, inner things come to outer expression, for out of the thoughts of the heart come murders, adulteries, and other evils (Mk. 7:20–23). The mere fact that the Bible often names the "inner" man by reference to bodily organs (heart, kidneys, liver) is a hint that Scripture does not sharply distinguish inner spiritual from outer physical realities; even the "inner" man is conceived physically, not as an unbodied, ghostly self.[8] Scripture thus teaches a complex interplay of inner/outer in human existence, a duality within unified human being. There is more to us than appears on the surface, but human being is always "being in the world" because it always means "being a body." Whatever else we might say about a baptized person, we can say with utter confidence that he is baptized, and this is an irreversible moment in his "being in the world."

Religion is private: This is the heresy of Christianity in a nutshell.

9

Even in their most conservative forms, rituals are often efforts to come to terms with the reality of change; funerals attempt to preserve or restore normalcy, but funerals occur only when normalcy has changed radically.

Many other rites have to do with creating new sets of relations rather than maintaining old ones. Wedding ceremonies do not guard the *status quo ante* but create a wholly new thing—a marriage—and confer, *ex opere operato*, a new identity upon a man and woman, the identity of husband and wife. Rites of inauguration, ordination, initiation are not merely about community "maintenance" or "preservation" but are equally concerned with changing what is.

Ritual is simultaneously conservative and revolutionary in the way carpentry is. Once you have mastered the technique of driving a nail, there is no reason to experiment with new ways of doing it; but you learn to drive nails because you want to build *new* things.

Far from yearning for a golden, changeless past, "ritualists" are the most progressive of men, fearlessly facing the unknown future so long as they can take along their prayer books and water, their wafers and their wine.

10

The Reformers saw the Reformation as a rediscovery of the newness of the New Covenant. For the Reformers, the medieval church was a tragic reversion to Old Covenant forms and an Old

Covenant theology of sacrifice and priesthood. From this perspective, the mainspring of the Reformation was not so much
the book of Romans as the book of Hebrews.

In his tract on "The Necessity of Reforming the Church,"[9]
Calvin attacked Rome for turning back the clock of redemptive
history. Rome required ceremonies that were Old Covenant in
origin and character, and much more drastically, the Roman
church understood the clergy as priests in the same sense as
Aaronic priests. Thus, Calvin complained of the number of ceremonies, the introduction of useless ceremonies, and the exter-
nalism that confused ceremonies with true piety. The Roman
church had instituted "a new Judaism" by inaugurating "numerous puerile extravagancies" and rites borrowed from paganism.
In the liturgy of the Supper, the Reformers discarded ceremonies partly because they were too many, and "partly because
some savoured too much of Judaism."

Despite similarities, Calvin said that the Reformers were not
like Israel's prophets. They differed in the fact that the prophets
denounced the abuse of divinely sanctioned ceremonies, while
the Reformers objected to invented ceremonies. Calvin continued,

> . . . our business had been to correct numerous rites which had
> either crept in through oversight, or had been turned to abuse;
> and which, moreover, by no means accorded with the time. For,
> if we would not throw every thing into confusion, we must
> never lose sight of the distinction between the old and new dis-
> pensations, and of the fact that ceremonies, the observance of
> which was useful under the law, are now not only superfluous,
> but vicious and absurd.

Christ abrogated ceremonies because "the body has been
manifested in Christ" and also because "God is now pleased to
instruct his church after a different manner." Citing Galatians
4:5 and Colossians 2:4, 14, 17, Calvin asks, "Since, then, God

has freed his church from the bondage which he had imposed upon it, can anything, I ask, be more perverse than for men to introduce a new bondage in place of the old?"

On these points, Calvin was both profoundly right and profoundly mistaken. He was correct because he had identified an important motif of late medieval Catholicism; there truly was a reversion to Old Covenant structures and a kind of Galatianism at work.[10] Priests had separated themselves from the people and saw themselves as sanctified with a holiness that, according to Paul, was the common possession of all who are in Christ the Priest. Rome had introduced ceremonies without divine authorization, leading people to search for blessing from God in cul-de-sacs and along avenues that God had not promised to bless.

On the other hand, Calvin was fatally wrong in suggesting that this Galatianism was found wherever there is an emphasis on ritual per se. Calvin notwithstanding, the redemptive-historical move that the New Testament announces is not from ritual to non-ritual, from an Old Covenant economy of signs to a New Covenant economy beyond signs. The movement instead is from rituals and signs of distance and exclusion (the temple veil, cutting of the flesh, sacrificial smoke ascending to heaven, laws of cleanliness) to signs and rituals of inclusion and incorporation (the rent veil, the common baptismal bath, the common meal).

Rituals are as essential to the New Covenant order as to the Old; they are simply *different* rituals.

11

There is a circular relationship between modernity's aversion to ritual and the Church's. The Reformation interpreted the progress of history as a movement from ritual to non-ritual, and this shaped a bias against ritual in the consciousness of the early modern Europe. This anti-ritual consciousness, radicalized and secularized, reinvaded the Church from which it had arisen.

12

J. P. S. Uberoi is almost correct that the modern world arose at Marburg: when Luther and Zwingli parted ways on sacramental theology, "symbol" went to Zurich and "reality" off to Wittenberg.

In fact, the sundering had taken place centuries earlier and has its source already in the patristic period, as soon as the notion of "sacraments" emerged, as soon as theologians formed the notion that "sacraments" were magically and ontologically different from other signs, and as soon as they came to believe that the Church's meal was a supernatural meal and the Church's water was supernatural water.

This conception of "sacraments," reinforced by Reformation and especially Reformed conceptions of ritual and redemptive history, bears significant responsibility for promoting the heresy of Christianity. If "sacraments" are completely different sorts of things from the signs and rituals of cultural life, then Christianity is something completely different from culture. It is a "religious" community, an island of sanctity and miracle surrounded by a sea of profane and mechanistic nature. "Sacraments" thus both misconstrue the nature of the Church and the nature of the world; by reserving "miracle" to the Church, "sacraments" leave the rest of creation to be run by "natural process."[11]

Sacraments grow out of and promote Christianity; and so I am against sacraments to the degree I am against Christianity.

On the other hand, ritual is public, and no ritualized religion can be completely privatized. Ritual is action, and no ritualized religion can be completely intellectualized. Ritual is communal, and no ritualized religion can be completely individualized.

Ritual is incompatible with Christianity; and so I am for Christian rituals to the degree I am against Christianity.

13

Liturgical theology is sometimes seen as the preserve of antiquarians and monks, cute and reassuring but irrelevant to the large issues of theology and to the mission of the Church. Nothing could be further from the truth.

Liturgical or ritual theology is one of the chief fronts in the Church's war against the heresy of Christianity.

Which is to say, liturgical theology is one of the chief fronts in the war against secular modernity.

14

Ritual reflects and shapes individual life and the order of a community. It is at the heart of Christian *paedeia*.

For individuals, Christian ritual trains the body and soul in suitable posture and movement.[12] By moving us through a series of spiritual and physical postures, liturgical ritual imposes a choreography on us. Patterned by rituals of worship, we begin to live life before God *as* kneeling to confess, *as* standing to hear, *as* singing and clapping in praise, *as* sitting to eat and drink. Worship trains us in the steps for walking, for dancing rightly through life. Christian cult trains us in the protocols of life in the presence of God, and thereby, since all life is in the presence of God, acclimates the worship to Christian culture.

For groups, ritual depicts the world as it ought to be, the real world as it is believed to be, especially the social and political realities of the world. Christian ritual displays the world as we believe and hope it one day will be. Ritual displays to public view who goes where, how each of us fits into the whole, how the members of the body are knit into one while yet remaining many, how the melodic lines of each individual life harmonize into a communal symphony. By repeated display, ritual reminds us again and again that this is the real world, objectively real outside our imaginations, and encourages us to live on the confidence that this is the real world.

Through rituals of worship, we begin to realize together who we are together: *of course*, we are a sinful people who needs to break away from the world, to make a weekly exodus from

Egypt; *of course*, we are an ignorant people who needs to be instructed and reminded each week of our language and our story; *of course*, we are the children of our heavenly Father, who has given all things freely in His Son and displays that gift in the gift of food; *of course*, we have been ingrafted into the community of the Trinity, for each worship service begins in the name of the Father and the Son and the Spirit, and ends with the triune name spoken over us.

Ritual is also movement and drama and music. It not only displays the world as it is/ought to be, but trains us as a body how to live these realities. We not only *learn* that we are a sinful people, but are trained to say confession, not only learn to give thanks for all things but actually practice giving thanks, not only learn that we are table fellows of Jesus but actually share in that table. We not only glimpse the harmony of God's Song, but become part of that Song.

15

Reformed Protestants generally adopt only one physical posture in worship—sitting to listen to a sermon—and therefore we are trained in only one spiritual posture. We are trained to accept as a matter of course that it is possible to *think* our way through life, all of life.

16

Surely rituals like baptism and the Supper are not essential to salvation? Surely God can work outside means?

Consider—begin with the observation that human being in the world takes place in a linguistic and symbolic medium. Individual experience and history are situated in this medium; language and other signifying processes of culture are always already there. We do not invent our own language; we learn an existing language and learn to name the world through that language. We do not establish our own complex of gestures and signs and rites of mannerly behavior; our parents impose them on us. Through this *paedeia*, we pick up the ticks and habits of ethnic, national, family, or religious identity. And those ticks and habits of language, thought, and action shape the way we experience the world and respond to it.

If this is the case, then to say that the Spirit "bypasses" created means and acts "directly" on us is to say that He bypasses history and normal human experience. And it follows that the *real* encounter with the Spirit takes place outside the compass of human being in the world, and this suggests that salvation is not a historical reality in any strong sense. If this is true, the Spirit works most powerfully (or only) in the mystical gaps and interstices of history, and this leaves vast reaches of life more or less beyond the operation of the Spirit. This is the heresy of Christianity.

Besides, what is salvation but life lived as it was meant to be lived, life lived now as it will one day be lived, in trust and obedience, in thankfulness and praise? Insofar as baptism and the Supper train us to live now as the eschatological humanity, insofar as they train us in the "postures" of Christian living, they are necessary to salvation. Insofar as baptism and the Supper mark and shape the community of the Church as a new humanity in Christ, just so far they are necessary to the saved life of the people of God.

17

This has become one of my favorite citations: when Aquinas considered the "necessity" of the sacraments, his answer cited Augustine's dictum (*Against Faustus* 19.11) that no religious body or group can exist without signs and symbols. Signs and rites are necessary because the Church is necessary, and the Church is necessary because salvation is a restoration of man not just in his individuality but in his social relations. The new creation must take a social form, and since there is no social interaction, common goals and programs, or harmonization of disparate melodies without the use of signs and symbols, common languages, common allegiances, and common participation in rites and ceremonies, so there can be no Church without sacraments.

Since there can be no salvation without the Church, since, indeed, the Church *is* salvation, there is no salvation without the sacraments.

18

Are baptism and the Supper symbols or realities?

It is a false question. Words are symbols, but we know that words have enormous power for good or evil. A flag, a handshake, a kiss, a poster, are also symbols but they are clearly as real as stars and snakes and salamanders. So, to say that the Church's bread, wine, and water are symbols is not to say that they are without value or power, or that they lack "reality." It is merely to say that whatever power they have is the kind of power that symbols have, and not the kind of power that a combustion engine or a nuclear power plant has. It is to say that whatever reality they have is the kind of reality that symbols always have. Theology goes into the ditch when it treats symbols as if they were something other than symbols. And at the bottom of that ditch is Christianity.

So, the opposition of symbol and reality is a false antithesis.

We can arrive at the same destination along another pathway. What is baptism? Not water only, not only water poured. Baptism is water poured on a person in obedience to Christ and by His authorization. What is the Supper? It is not just bread and wine, and not just eating of bread and wine. It is eating bread and wine by members of Christ's body at Christ's invitation. Christ's authorization and definition and invitation make all the difference.

Baptism is not a "symbol" of someone becoming a disciple. Because Jesus designated it as such, this symbol *is* his "becoming-a-disciple." It is not a picture of a man being joined in covenant to Christ; it *is* a man being joined in covenant to Christ.

The Supper is not a symbol of a meal with Jesus. The bread and wine are symbols of Christ's body and blood, but because Jesus promised to be with us at the table, this symbolic meal *is* a meal with Jesus. By eating the symbols, we are partaking the reality.

Symbol or reality? It is a false question.

19

Public and social symbols do not function in abstraction from instruction, teaching, or (if you will) indoctrination. The significance Americans attach to the American flag or the "Star-Spangled Banner"—the emotions these symbols call up, the sense of unity they evoke, the actions they encourage—are not detached from our instruction in American history, our memories of life in America, the stated goals and aspirations of the American experiment. So also, the public symbols and rituals of the Church have their significance within a pattern of instruction. This does not make the symbols superfluous, meaningless or ineffective, nor does it mean that baptism and the Supper are no more than appendixes to the Word. In the context of instruction in the Word, water, bread, and wine are effective signs in making the Church a distinct people.

20

At the spatial center of the ancient city was the *agora*, which was consecrated not only for the political business of the city but for its religious business. Especially, the *agora*—the high city or acropolis—was devoted to festival. As Paul Cartledge has put it, "religious festivals were indeed the beating heart of ancient Greek religion, and festivals somehow linking centre and periphery thus perform a vital civic political function."[13] The *polis* was in fact formed as a political institution by the unification of the cults of the various "houses" or villages that constituted it. As in the home, the center of the city was a common hearth-fire.

For the Greeks, time was organized by festivals to various gods: "There were twelve months, each divided into three groups of ten days; the individual months were generally named after a festival celebrated during that month."[14] Festivals normally began with lively processions and included sacrifices followed by meals, competitive performances of drama and recitations of epic poetry (especially Homer), hymn-singing, prayers and other acts of homage to the gods, and often games.

Poetic recitations and dramatized myths presented the values of the city, and the distribution of sacrificial meat manifested its internal structure. According to Simon Price's description of the Panathenaia,

> The cattle bought with rent from land sacred to Athena, once they had reached the Akropolis, were sacrificed on the great altar of Athena in front of the Pantheon, with the finest reserved for a sacrifice on the nearby altar of Athena Nike "Victory." The sacrificial meat from two of the sacrifices was distributed there to various civic officials and participants in the sacrifice: the prutaneis, the chief magistrates, the treasurer of the goddess, the sacrificial officials, the board of generals and division commanders and also Athenians who participated in the procession and the maidens who acted as kanephoroi (Vessel Bearers). The meat from the other sacrifices was distributed to the Athenian people in the vicinity of the Pompeion, portions assigned to each deme in proportion to the number of participants in the procession from that deme. That is, under a democratic system all citizens were eligible to a portion of the sacrificial meal, at public expense. Honoured civic officials (numbering up to sixty-six) dined in special rooms inside the Pompeion. Formal rules, varying from cult to cult, specified who could participate in the sacrifice. Sacred officials (both male and female) would receive their perquisites; both men and women attending the festival might receive portions of the roast meat. The rules

were thus a reflection of the social groupings involved in a particular cult.[15]

Common participation in the sacrificial meal thus set out the boundaries of the *polis*, and the specific portions were distributed in accord with the standing of various participants. The animal's body was a symbol of the social body, and its distribution a symbol of the community (*koinonia*, used for festival meals) of the many formed into one body. Feasts traced the contours of the city—by including some and excluding others, the festival established an in-group and an out-group, and by the distribution of food and seating arrangements, it presented the internal structure of the city.

Similar patterns are evident in private Roman banquets. For Romans, the *cena* or dinner was not a family meal, as it is, even now, for many Americans. Instead, it was often and normatively a meal of men, which excluded children and wives. Being given a place at the table was a sign of inclusion in the host's circle, and the arrangement of guests displayed the rankings in that circle. Patron-client relations were displayed and reinforced at table, and dinners "allowed the opportunity . . . for a spectacular display of authority and power, which could be carefully orchestrated before a select audience of people."[16] The results could be insulting; Martial complained about the inequities of the menu:

> Since I am asked to dinner, no longer, as before, a purchased guest [i.e., a client], why is not the same dinner served to me as to you? You take oysters fattened in the Lucrine lake, I suck a mussel through a hole in the shell; you get mushrooms, I take hog-fungus; you tackle turbot, but I brill. Golden with fat, a turtledove gorges you with its bloated rump; there is set before me a magpie that has died in its cage. Why do I dine without you, even though, Ponticus, I am dining with you? The dole has gone; let us have the benefit of it—let us eat the same fare.[17]

Imperial banquets, which were religious as well as social occasions, displayed the order of Roman society and of politics. Attention was focused on the emperor, who sometimes reclined
godlike in an apse at the head of the table, elevated above the
guests, with his favorites grouped in ranks around him.[18] The
emperor's preference for certain guests was also evident in
apophoreton, a cultic term that originally referred to sacrificial
portions given to guests to "carry away" from a religious meal
and later came to refer to a host's parting gifts to his guests.[19]
Throughout the Roman empire, moreover, imperial religion was
celebrated in city festivals of sacrifice, games, and processions
that provided a microcosm of the Roman world and inculcated
respect for Roman power.[20]

The political importance of festivals and public ritual was not
lost on the ancients. Solon was truly a Greek Moses, not only
organizing the Athenian legal system but also a cycle of sacrificial
feasts, and he enlisted the help of Epimenides, "the seventh wise
man," who contributed to "purifying and sanctifying the city, by
certain propitiatory and expiatory lustrations, and foundations
of sacred buildings, by that means making them more submissive
to justice, and more inclined to harmony."[21] Plato saw it as the
duty of a legislator to establish temples and rituals in accord
with oracular direction—the city should observe whatever "ancient tradition has sanctioned in whatever manner, whether by
apparitions or reputed inspiration of Heaven, in obedience to
which mankind have established sacrifices in connection with
mystic rites" (*Laws*, 738).

When the Church entered the Greco-Roman world, then,
she encountered a world awash in civic-religious feasts, and one
of the first things she did was to set up a new feast, a new sacrifice, a new set of civic-religious rituals governed by different
manners and protocols. In this, the Church was simply following
her Jewish predecessor. Israel was also a nation organized and
bounded by festivals. Her calendar was a calendar of feasts and

sacrifices (Lev. 23; Num. 28–29), and her identity as the people of the exodus was annually reaffirmed by the Passover celebration. As a ritual and symbol of initiation, circumcision marked the Jew in the flesh as an alien to the Greco-Roman world. An autonomous *politeuma* within the Greco-Roman *polis*, the Jews of the diaspora observed their own cycle of feasts and holidays.

By setting up a new festival alongside the Jewish synagogue and Greek city, the Church established an alternative *agora* and marked out new contours of civic order. Baptism marked out the borders of the new city, which welcomed Jews and Gentiles; the Supper reinforced the baptismal boundary between in-group (church) and out-group (world) and reconfigured the shape of table fellowship.

21

A test for your local church: which holiday receives more attention, the Fourth of July or Ascension? Mother's Day or Pentecost?

Now, why is that?

22

The festive center of the Church did not begin with Jesus' ascension or the outpouring of the Spirit. Years before the disciples broke bread on Pentecost, the kingdom of God had already erupted into the world as a new festival that ritualized a new story, which was the story of a new city. Jesus, after all, came eating and drinking, in all the wrong ways and with all the wrong people.

Jesus ate with the wrong *people*, thus establishing the theology of baptism.

Jesus *ate* with the wrong people, thus establishing the theology of the Supper.

23

Baptism forms as well as symbolizes the new city of God. Through baptism, all sorts and conditions of men are made members of one body and become citizens of a single community.

Symbol or reality? It is a false question.

24

Paul said that the "least seemly" members were to be welcomed and honored in the Church more than those who have their own seemliness (1 Cor. 12:12–27). The weak, broken, immature, disgusting, and despised are embraced as productive members of the body—so long as they confess Jesus as Lord.

Can we ritualize that truth about the Church on Baptist principles? Can we say we accept the "unseemly" and "weak," while applying baptism only to articulate adults? Does not the Baptist practice of baptism send a very different, even pagan, message?

25

The Reformers cut through the lush overgrowth of subordinate rituals that had clustered around baptism and reduced the rite to its biblical form—a sprinkling with water. That was right and proper. Yet, most of those sub-rites presented the truth about the event of baptism: it really is a renunciation of the world, a deliverance from the domain of Satan into the domain of Christ, an investiture with royal and priestly garments. Though we ought not add rites to the water of baptism, we must learn that the water is thick with these associations and meanings.

26

Many Christians say we cannot be sure that anything has changed once someone is baptized. What are we saying?

In baptism, God marks me as His own, with His name. God makes me a member of His household, the Church. If we say nothing important has happened we are suggesting that we have some identity that is more fundamental than God's name for us, some self that is beyond God's capacity to claim and name.

"Of course," we object, "God says I am in His family, a son, but I'm really something else." That is a most egregious claim to autonomy: I yam who I yam regardless of who God says I yam.

It may turn out, of course, that God's final name for a baptized person is "prodigal son."

27

Private dinners in the Greco-Roman world were used to inflate the honor of the patron and frequently displayed social divisions in the arrangement and fare of the meal. Pliny was opposing a common custom when he complained that the host of one banquet and his social equals were given fine food and wine, while those of lower social status were seated at a separate table and given ordinary food and bad wine.[22]

The Corinthians were, in short, simply following standard custom when they introduced social and other divisions into the meal.

But Paul condemned this "standard custom."

Paul did not permit the Corinthians to organize their festivals like the banquets of Roman aristocrats. He did not allow the rich and powerful to take the head seats at the table. He insisted that the meal of the new city should reflect the civic order of the new city. The meal of the new city manifests the perichoretic unity of the members of the Church in one another, which reflects and participates in the eternal perichoretic *koinonia* of Father, Son, and Spirit.

28

We are what we eat.

In contrast to the animal sacrifices of the Old Covenant and of Greco-Roman festivals, the Christian feast is a feast of bread

and wine, both cultivated foods, products of culture. The stuff of
the meal thus signals that the community is a "construct," not a
"natural" community, a "fictive" kin group rather than a kin
group bound by flesh and blood.[23] (The Christian household is
bound together by blood, but it is blood *shed* not blood transmit-
ted in birth.) Bread and wine thus signal that this table fellowship is one where there is neither Jew nor Greek, Scythian nor
Cretan, slave nor free.

The Supper made fascism discernible and exposed the injus-
tice of the ideology of blood and soil. Prior to the Supper and
before the Church, fascism was simple common sense.

The Church attacked this kind of common sense.

Because we are what we eat.

29

We are together how and what we eat together. But we don't eat
together.

Is it any wonder that we are not together?

30

Romans normally excluded children from the dinner table until
the age of fifteen or sixteen, at which age boys received the *toga
virilis* that marked their entrance to manhood. Family dinner as
we know it, with parents and children at a single table, was a
Christian invention, not some "natural" form of family life.[24] The
family dinner is a reflection of the eucharistic meal, the meal
that welcomed all members of Christ to the table.

Opposition to communion of children is pagan and seeks to
reverse the revolutionary table fellowship established by the
Church. It is an attempt to return to Egypt.

31

All members of Christ are welcomed to the table—that is the
point. The point of the Supper is to overturn all other sorts and

conditions of table fellowship, all table fellowship that would exclude the lowly or puff up the high and mighty. And in overturn-
ing such table fellowship, the gospel overturns all such social
orders and establishes the Church's own order as the true social
order.

Symbol or reality?

Any notion of a distinction between the "symbol" and the "reality" collapses entirely.

For the "symbolic" common meal *is* the reality aimed at.

4

Against Ethics

1

Transformation of life, including social and political life, is not an "implication" of the gospel. That would suggest that the gospel is over "here," and that it has implications for life which are over "there." It would mean that the gospel is on the left hand, and that we can draw out the moral implications of the gospel on the right hand. Such a procedure is compatible with heresy of Christianity with its separation of "theology" and "practice," but it is not a biblical picture.

Transformation of life is not an implication of the gospel but inherent in the gospel, because the good news is *about* transformation of life.

2

By the time Paul wrote 2 Corinthians, his apostleship had come under suspicion from some within the Corinthian church and Paul was forced to mount a defense of his calling.[1] Some Corinthians charged that Paul was acting according to the "flesh," that is, according to worldly motives and selfish standards, instead of by the Spirit's direction (1:17; cf. 10:2). The basis for this charge was the apparent vacillation in Paul's travel plans. He had stated his intention to pass through Corinth both on his way into Macedonia and again on his way back toward Judea, but he changed plans and did not go through Corinth

(1:15–16). His opponents seized upon this, arguing that Paul could not be trusted since he said "Yes" one minute and "No" the next. No one guided by the Spirit would be this fickle.

Though this seems a trivial point, Paul took the charge seriously. He realized that if he could not be trusted with travel plans, he could not be trusted with the gospel. When Paul wrote, "our word to you is not yes and no" (1:18), he referred both to his missionary itinerary and his message. His underlying assumption was that there must be a correspondence between life and message, and, more particularly, between speech in daily life and speech in the *ekklesia*. Both Paul and his opponents accepted this premise; both agreed that if one is unreliable in daily life and speech, his preaching had to be unreliable. Genuine apostles were not just carriers of the gospel; they had to embody the gospel.

Later in the epistle, Paul generalized the point. For all the Church, words are to be *yes* or *no*, not *yes* and *no*. This point is central to Paul's description of the New Covenant in 2 Corinthians 3, which continues Paul's defense of his apostleship. Again, Paul treated the situation as a trial and presented evidence to defend his claim to status as a minister of the New Covenant. Specifically, he offered, as a letter of commendation, the Corinthian church herself. The fact that a church had sprouted up in Corinth when Paul preached the gospel proved that he was a minister of the Spirit. The very existence of the church was a sign that through Paul the Spirit was writing on tablets of the human heart (3:3). Paul's reference to the tablets of the heart in contrast to tablets of stone echoes passages from the prophets, which speak about the future coming of a new covenant (Jer. 31:33; Ezek. 36:26–27). Paul claimed to be part of the fulfillment of these promises, ministering the Spirit that renews hearts.

Paul made much the same point in contrasting his own ministry with that of Moses. After being on the mountain, Moses

came down reflecting the glory of Yahweh that he had seen. Yet
the people could not gaze on the glory and Moses had to veil his
face. The reason for this, Paul said, was the hardness of the
people's hearts; Israel, not Moses, was the problem (3:14). Now
in the New Covenant, however, the problem of hardness of heart
has been solved, since the Spirit has been poured out to write
the law on the hearts of those who believe in Jesus. As a result,
Paul could minister without a veil, with open face. Before, hard-
hearted Israel had to turn from the glory; now, with hearts made
new by the Spirit, the Corinthians can gaze into the face of the
glory of God in Jesus and be transformed from glory to glory.

That *is* the message of the gospel. Transformation from glory
to glory is the impossible reality that the gospel of the New Covenant announces and effects. The gospel is about the transformation of hearts and lives, the announcement that the promises of
the prophets have now been fulfilled in Jesus and the Spirit.

We might be tempted to say that the message of the gospel is
true, whether or not there are any apparent effects when it is
preached. "Of course," we think, "we must make every effort to
ensure that our lives are consistent with that truth, but even if
we are inconsistent, it is true nonetheless."

That is wrong-headed. It reduces the gospel to a philosophical
viewpoint, another belief system that is tested by logical coher-
ence. To approach the gospel in this way is to propound Christianity.

And that is not an option that Paul allowed. Paul did not agree
that the gospel would be true even if no one lived out of the gospel. Paul's gospel had an empirical test built into it; if no one was
transformed, then the message that announced the transformation could not possibly be true. The first and chief defense of the
gospel, the first "letter of commendation" not only for Paul but
for Jesus, is not an argument but the life of the Church conformed to Christ by the Spirit in service and suffering. A community of sinners whose corporate life resembles Christ—that

is the Church's first apologetic. The very existence of such a city is our main "argument."

3

But does she exist?

4

The New Testament does not present an ethical system in our modern sense or even in the ancient Aristotelian sense.[2] It is not ethics in our modern sense because the apostles taught that right living was impossible without the Spirit and outside the community of the Spirit. In one respect, Paul is rather close to Aristotle. Aristotle claimed that the location of the good life was always the city-state, that "ethics" was a subdivision of "politics." And, despite the significant changes that took place in the structure and status of the city-state between Aristotle and the first century, the *polis* was still the imaginary setting for ethical reflection among philosophers in Paul's day. The early church agreed in principle: living well, living according to the will of God, meant living within the Christian *polis*. By contrast, much modern ethics is taught as if individual monads of humanity, living on desert islands, make ethical decisions about specific problematic issues, without help or insight from anybody else.

Modern ethics, further, especially in America, is an effort to speak to issues of right and wrong without mentioning God, or at least without mentioning any specific god. Ethics, in other words, operates completely within the confinements of liberal order, which attempts to cleanse the public realm (including the realm of ethical debate) of particular theological claims. Ethics is an effort to find a language for obligation without reference to Jesus. Clearly, Paul could not begin to countenance such a project.

But Paul and the other apostles were not teaching ethics even in the Aristotelian sense because they did not slice up human existence in the way Aristotle did. Aristotle assumed there is a clear boundary between the realm of "practice," which has to do with human actions that remain part of the actor, and "poesis" or "making," which has to do with human actions that produce something external to the actor. Thus, for Aristotle, the exercise of prudence is within the realm of "practice," while making a piece of furniture is "poetic." Ethics, for Aristotle, has to do with the former realm, with practice, but not with poesis. If this is true, then ethics remains a discipline concerned with individual and internal realities. Despite Aristotle's claim that the *polis* is the arena in which the ethical life is lived, ethics as reflection on practice ultimately has to do with what is mine and mine only. As soon as I produce something in the public realm, then I am no longer in the realm of practice, and no longer doing something encompassed by ethics.

For Paul, the transformation of life can never remain "mine and mine alone" because it originates in the Spirit who works through the gospel, and because it radiates in glory. For Paul, as soon as we begin to practice we break out in poetry.

Further, Paul was not talking about ethics in an Aristotelian sense because Aristotle, though hardly an advocate of a warrior ethic, still understood virtue in heroic terms. Virtue, *arete*, originally meant victory in a conflict, and in Aristotle's case the conflict was between reason and passion. Virtue is the triumph of reason over passion and appetite. For Paul (as for Augustine and Aquinas), virtue is fundamentally charity, fundamentally an outflow that tends to break all bounds and confinements. Virtue is trinitarian, reflecting the eternal ecstasy, the flowing out of the Father into the Son into the Spirit into the Son into the Father.

Christians fall into ethics only if they have already embraced Christianity, only if they believe that Christian faith and morals are private and individual. If we are to be against Christianity, we must also be against ethics.

5

Plutarch wrote, "God offers himself to all as a pattern of every excellence, thus rendering human virtue, which is in some sort an assimilation to himself, accessible to all who can follow God."[3]

Christians agreed and joined the issue at the level of theology, asking, Who is God? How does He act? In contrast to the self-absorbed deities of the myths, the God revealed in Jesus Christ was a Trinity, a community of self-giving love. Conforming one's life and one's community to the pattern of excellence found in *this* God had very different results from conforming life and community to Zeus.[4]

Conversion from idol worship to the worship of the living God thus involved a complete transformation of outlook and imagination and action. Changing the object of worship meant changing the entire direction and orientation of life. The character of the liturgy molded the character of the liturgical community; what was done and who was worshiped in the assembly determined what kind of city would be formed around the assembly.

6

In the recent film *The Others*, the house belongs to the dead. The living are the intruders. That is a perfect summation of the ethos of ancient paganism, for which the ancestral ways always provide the final touchstone.

Ephesians rioted when a new doctrine was preached, when some intruders showed up urging people to abandon the ways of their fathers (Acts 19). So did the Jews of Jerusalem (Acts 21).

7

Whereas the God of Israel is not the God of the dead but of the living. For His city, the future is always the touchstone. His city now is not a preserve of the city of yesterday but an anticipation of the city of tomorrow.

8

John Milbank argues that both ancient paganism and its post-modern counterpart are founded on what he calls an "ontology of violence." In ancient Greek culture, this was manifested in several ways: the gods of the Greek myths do not "create" but merely control chaos through violence; the highest principle of Greek philosophy is either chaos or some dialectic between chaos and order, but this latter dualism necessarily rests on a more fundamental conflict; and this means that political order is essentially a matter of controlling violence through the use of counterviolence.[5] Myths of violence formed the ethos and structures of the Greco-Roman city.

Stanley Hauerwas has written,

> These rites, baptism and Eucharist, are not just "religious things" that Christian people do. They are the essential rituals of our politics. Through them we learn who we are. Instead of being motives or causes for effective social work on the part of Christian people, these liturgies *are* our effective social work. For if the Church *is* rather than has a social ethic, these actions are our most important social witness. It is in baptism and the Eucharist that we see most clearly the marks of God's kingdom in the world. They set our standard, as we try to bring every aspect of our lives under their sway.[6]

Citing 1 Corinthians 11:17–26, Hauerwas makes the point that there can be no separation between "being a holy people" and "being a sacramental people": "Our eating with our Lord is not different from our learning to be his disciples, his holy people."[7] In the Church, the wealthy and refined were *required* to eat with the vulgar poor, and this could not help but challenge and re-make the way they "leaned into life."

In short, the ethos of the Christian Church was formed by the Spirit, working through the Church's myth and rituals, just as the ethos of the Greek *polis* and the empire of Rome had been

formed by demons, telling different myths and binding worshipers to themselves through different rituals.

9

Though by the first century the age of heroes was a dim
memory, the ethos of Rome and its empire was a magnification
of the heroic ethic. The agonistic dimensions of Greek virtue
(*arete*) were still apparent in Roman *virtus*, now translated into
an imperial project. Shame for the Romans was the great evil,
while self-glorification, honor, and praise the great good.

This, at least, is how Augustine described his pagan Roman
predecessors and many of his contemporaries. What especially
characterized the ancient Romans was devotion to glory: "It was
for this that they desired to live, for this they did not hesitate to
die." For Augustine, the Roman love of glory was a political as
well as a moral "virtue." Romans "felt it would be shameful for
their own country to be enslaved, but glorious for her to have
dominion and empire; so they set their hearts first on making
her free, then on making her sovereign." Hence, the whole political history of Rome may be traced to this one "splendid vice."
It left Romans itching for enemies. Sallust, for instance,

> praises Caesar, among other things, for his ambition for a great
> command, for an army, for a new war in which his abilities
> could shine. Thus the chief desire of men of eminent qualities
> was that Bellona should arouse wretched nations to war and
> drive them on with her bloody whip to give an occasion for the
> abilities to shine.[8]

Augustine recognized a difference between the lust for glory
and the desire for domination, the *libido dominandi*. The former
was a desire to be judged well by men, and the latter simply a
desire for power. While the desire for glory was itself a vice, it
had a effect of suppressing other, more damaging faults: "This
unbounded passion for glory, above all else, checked their other

appetites."[9] Achieving glory depended on being well regarded by others, and this desire for good reputation leads men to aim at least for the appearance of virtue. Some Romans, however, were eager only for domination and were therefore "worse than the beasts": "If anyone aims at power and domination without that kind of desire for glory which makes a man fear the disapprobation of sound judges, then he generally seeks to accomplish his heart's desire by the most barefaced crimes."[10]

Augustine was duly impressed with Rome's achievement. He recounts in some detail the heroism of Rome's great men, their willingness to suffer to make Rome the dominant city of the world, their renunciation of comforts and pleasures. All this is a lesson for Christians: "If we do not display, in the service of the most glorious City of God, the qualities of which the Romans, after their fashion, gave us something of a model, in their pursuit of the glory of their earthly city, then we must feel the prick of shame."[11]

Yet, on the basis of Roman conceptions of honor, there could be no community, nothing really common among men. Augustine suggested that "A people is the association of a multitude of rational beings united by a common agreement on the objects of their love." By this definition, Rome had never been a people or a commonwealth. True commonwealth exists only where

> God, the one supreme God, rules an obedient City according to his grace, forbidden sacrifice to any save himself alone; and where in consequence[12] the soul rules the body in all men who belong to this City and obey God, and the reason faithfully rules the vices in a lawful system of subordination; so that just as the individual righteous man lives on the basis of faith and is active in love, so the association of people, of righteous men lives on the same basis of faith, active in love, the love with which a man loves God as God ought to be loved, and loves his neighbor as himself.

Outside a *polis* devoted to love of God, there is no justice and therefore no commonwealth. Indeed, there is no virtue: "Although the virtues are reckoned by some people to be genuine and honourable when they are related only to themselves and are sought for no other end, even then they are puffed up and proud, and so are to be accounted vices rather than virtues."[13]

Rome was no commonwealth for another reason as well. When each is striving for his own glory, there can be no "common agreement on the objects of love." Each man loves himself, and the city fragments into hundreds and thousands of *micropoleis*. It is no surprise that Rome's internal history was a history of strife, and that the Roman people could be united only when they were faced with a common enemy. This, Augustine points out, was what brought the clashes of plebeian and patrician to an end—the threat from Carthage.[14] No wonder Romans itched for enemies.

10

Ramsay Macmullen has considered the Roman notion of *dignitas*, which was not only a value and character trait but a set of social practices embedded in Roman social structure. For the "Haves" of the Roman empire, *dignitas* was displayed in "the parade of wealth, the shouting herald who went first in the street, the showy costume and large retinue, the holding of oneself apart, and the limitation of familiar address." By the same token, *dignitas*, for Roman writers, "meant the ability to defend one's display by force if need be; to strike back at anyone who offended one or hurt one or offended one's dependents; to avenge oneself and others, and to be perceived as capable of all such baneful, alarming conduct."[15]

The city was the political context for these displays of *dignitas*. As Wayne Meeks has written,

> Honor and shame were as ubiquitous in the life of a rural clan as in an urban household. Nevertheless, the polis provided the

most conspicuous stages on which the daily rituals of patronage and friendship were acted out. It was in the polis that the great man paraded to his bath with crowds of dependents and slaves as his entourage. It was in the polis that statues and steles and inscriptions on public buildings proclaimed the benefactions of the most-honored. It was in the city that seating at a dinner party graphed out the status of those present.[16]

Under the system known as "patronage" or "clientalia," these displays were carried by "clients" to enhance the dignity of their "patrons." Wes Howard-Brook describes the patronage system, highlighting its mythical underpinnings:

> In a nutshell [the patronage system] generated a pyramidal set of social and economic relations. At the top, of course, were the wealthy elite—members of the Roman equestrian and senatorial classes. Persons below this narrow group linked with their "superiors" by exchanging *honor and loyalty* for access to *material resources*. This principle of exchange continued all the way through the society from the emperor to the lowest plebeian. . . . The entire patronage system was seen as supported by a plethora of divine beings, each "blessing" specific gatherings, places, and relationships. The patronage system was understood as simply a mirror of the relationships among the gods and goddesses themselves, with Zeus/Jupiter parallel to the emperor and with other parallels down the line.[17]

In these ways, Roman ethos of honor were writ into the fabric of social life throughout the empire and its cities.

11

And the apostle went up to the town square, and after he sat down, the disciples came to him.

And opening his mouth, he began to teach them, saying,

"You have heard that it was said, 'There is no one so wild as not to be greatly moved by the fear of reproach and dishonor.'

But I say to you, Follow our Lord Jesus, who despised shame, and consider yourselves worthy to suffer shame for His sake.

"You have heard that it was said, 'It is well if you yearn for praise from men.' But I say to you, Each man's praise will come to him from God.

"You have heard that it was said, 'Cruelty is not broken but fed by the tears of a supplicant.' But I say to you, Put on a heart of compassion, kindness, humility, gentleness, and patience.

"You have heard that it was said, 'Confession is both base and dangerous, and there is nothing worse than confession. Confession is a last resort.' But I say to you, Confess your sins one to another."

And when he had finished speaking, the disciples were astonished at his teaching. For he spake not as the Romans.[18]

12

Greek gods set their favor on the cunning, the strong, the brave, the beautiful. Even in Israel, only physically perfect priests could approach the altar and minister in Yahweh's house (Lev. 21–22).

Pharisees sought places of honor in the synagogue, a Jewish form of the Greco-Roman struggle for status.

Whereas Jesus sent His disciples out into the highways and byways to gather the lame, the blind, the halt, and the outcasts, in order to make them table-fellows in the kingdom and ministers in His Church. And James says, "Has not God chosen the poor?"

And yet, here are the disciples quarreling over their status and yearning for places of honor.

13

Few Christians have been as astute readers of Paul as Nietzsche. Pagan that he was, he could see what Paul was up to. He could see that Paul was slyly going about the business of "transvaluating all values," at least pagan ones, giving new names to old virtues and encouraging as virtue behavior once considered disgraceful.

14

Consider forgiveness. As the "chosen of God," Christians are called to "bear with one another, and forgive each other" (Col. 3:12–13). Try that in a patronage system, where your status and power depends on honor shown by clients and maintaining your *fama* (reputation) before your fellows and lashing out quickly against insult. In such a system, to absorb a slight is to expose yourself to disaster; to forgive an insult, a social and political impossibility; to turn the other cheek, unthinkable. Thus Jesus' sermon pulls out the cornerstones of *Romanitas*.

Take joy: Pressured by the need to maintain face, at the mercy of unpredictable gods, how could a pagan rejoice? Festivity was common, but not joy. As C. S. Lewis said, the gospel was too glad to be true.

Take humility: As Paul made clear throughout his correspondence with the Corinthians, conformity to Christ means conformity to His self-sacrifice and death. Paul's apostleship involved him in constant trouble, persecution, affliction for the sake of the churches and for the sake of the gospel (cf. 2 Cor. 11), and all believers were to imitate Christ by imitating Paul. Transformation into an image of the glory of God means conformity to the cross; it means self-sacrificing love; it means being caught up into the fellowship of self-giving love that is the triune communion. "Nonsense," sniffed the senator through his noble Roman nose.

15

Paul was not an ethicist, but Paul did encourage a particular ethos in the Church, and this ethos was to be embodied in the structures that gave shape to the Church's living-together.

The Pauline image of the Church as a body is found already in Aristotle and Stoic philosophers, and some of the vocabulary that clusters around Paul's presentation is also found in Aristotle.[19] When Paul wrote of the "proper working of each individual part" of the body (Eph. 4:16), he used the Greek word *meros* ("part"), a term used by Aristotle to describe the citizens of the commonwealth (*Politics* 1328a–b). Here, as elsewhere, the radical difference between Pauline and Aristotelian community is evident. For Aristotle, the *citizens* constitute the "parts" of the community, but in addition to the citizens, the city is populated by women, slaves, children, artisans and others who existed solely for the comfort and aid of the citizens (the *sine qua non*). Between the parts and the *sine qua non*, there is no chiasm of giving and receiving and giving again; the *meres* give and receive among themselves, but the *sine qua non* do nothing but give of themselves to make the life of citizens happy and noble. For Aristotle, since politics, the art of ruling and being ruled, is the goal of life, non-citizens who do not participate in politics— women, slaves, children—are less than fully human.[20]

In the Church, such a bifurcation between *meres* and others would not merely be unfortunate; it would be apostasy, as Paul emphasized when he berated the Corinthians for their factions and divisions, and Peter for refusing to eat with Gentiles. In Ephesians 4, it is clear that *every* part has his or her unique role to play in causing "the growth of the body for the building up of itself in love" (v. 16). Even the most "unseemly" members have their place in the body, their gifts to be used for the edification of the whole (1 Cor. 12). Within the Church, the chiasm encompasses the whole people; all are involved in continual and mutual giving and receiving and giving again, in imitation of the eternal fellowship of giving and receiving that constitutes the life of the Trinity, made possible by the New Covenant gift of the Spirit. Through the Spirit the Church is formed as the corporate embodiment of the self-gift of Christ.

16

There were some anticipations of the mutuality of the Christian *ekklesia* in Greek culture. Societies of friends were based on a mutual sharing among members; the Church is a community of friends.

And, the community of the dead was supposed by Greeks to be more egalitarian than the community of the living. The Church fulfills this vision also, since the Church is the community of the Risen Jesus, the city established on the far side of death.

17

The Church's life is essentially mission. More theologically, the life of God is mutual intertrinitarian mission and ministry, expressed economically as the Father sending the Son and Spirit to create and recreate the world. Since the Church is the community caught up through the Spirit into the community of God, the Church is also the mission caught up through the Spirit into the mission of God.[21]

18

Rodney Stark quotes from a Christian writer, Dionysius of Alexandria, who described the response of Christians to a plague in that city:

> Most of our brother Christians showed unbounded love and loyalty, never sparing themselves and thinking only of one another. Heedless of danger, they took charge of the sick, attending to their every need and ministering to them in Christ, and with them departed this life serenely happy. . . . Many, in nursing and curing others, transferred their death to themselves and died in their stead. . . . The best of our brothers lost their lives in this manner, a number of presbyters, deacons, and laymen winning high commendation so that death in this form, the result of great piety and strong faith, seems in every way the equal of martyrdom.[22]

By contrast, Dionysius said, "The heathen behaved in the very opposite way. At the first onset of the disease, they pushed the sufferers away and fled from their dearest, throwing them into the roads before they were dead and treated unburied corpses as dirt, hoping thereby to avoid the spread and contagion of the fatal disease; but do what they might, they found it difficult to escape." Even Galen, the celebrated physician who was living in Rome during an epidemic under Marcus Aurelius, fled the city to Asia Minor.

Even the Church's opponents commented on the strikingly different lives of Christians. Julian the Apostate marveled at Christian "benevolence toward strangers and care for the graves of the dead," and he recognized that the pagans showed no similar benevolence: "I think that when the poor happened to be neglected and overlooked by the priests, the impious Galileans observed this and devoted themselves to benevolence." And, "The impious Galileans support not only their poor, but ours as well, everyone can see that our people lack aid from us."[23]

19

Christian myth and ritual shape the people of God, by the power of the Spirit, into conformity to Christ, creating within the Church a palpable aroma of love, peace, purity, joy, ministry, mission and forgiveness. That aroma spreads from the Church to the city around it.

But what has happened if Christians fail to produce this aroma? What can we say when the fruits of the Spirit are not evident? What can we say when it no longer seems that the Spirit catches up the Church into the love and mission of the Trinity?

Perhaps the Spirit has departed. Perhaps the Spirit has been grieved.

20

Philotimia, love of honor, was the atmosphere of Roman life, the ethos in which Romans, especially the Roman aristocracy, lived and moved.

By contrast, the ground-motif of American life is freedom, self-generation, doing what we want. "Americans," Dinesh D'Souza tells us, "live in a nation where the life of the citizens is largely *self-directed.* The central goal of American freedom is self-reliance: the individual is placed in the driver's seat of his own life . . . . The self-directed life . . . seeks virtue—virtue realized not through external command but, as it were, 'from within.'"[24]

In this respect, America reflects the direction of modernity as a whole, a direction exemplified in the work of Oscar Wilde. In Philip Rieff's reading, Wilde envisioned a culture in which individuals would be freed from all inhibition and all authority, free to make what they want of themselves.[25] Every possibility would remain an open possibility.

Against Wilde's idea of the "primacy of possibility," Rieff insists that authoritative limits are of the essence of culture; culture requires "the primacy of interdiction" or prohibition. Every culture faces the threat of "sheer possibility," the danger that its members will agree with Ivan Karamazov's suggestion that "all is permitted." Cultures survive, Rieff argues, "only so far as the members of the culture learn, through their membership, how to narrow the range of choices otherwise open. Safely inside their culture—more precisely, the culture safely inside them—members of it are disposed to enact only certain possibilities of behavior while refusing even to dream of others." Thus, "members of the same culture can expect each other to behave in certain ways and not in others."[26]

Culture and character and common life are, in short, founded on prohibition, and this is true for every culture. What was interdicted may become permissible, but the new "permissiveness" generates prohibitions of its own. (Note the intolerance for Christian morality in our nation today.) Political revolutions are little more than glorified palace coups. Real revolutions are changes in patterns of moral demands. Cultural change is a change in "law."

Rieff's characterization of cultural revolution illuminates many aspects of the New Testament. Jesus' activities were consciously calculated to challenge Jewish notions of holiness, held explicitly by the Pharisees but embraced more loosely by many within first-century Palestine. Jesus ate and drank with tax collectors and sinners not only to demonstrate the scope of God's love, but also to challenge Pharisaical legalisms about tithing and food preparation. Jesus' practice thus set out a new pattern of interdictions and permissions, one founded on the idea that holiness demands mercy.[27]

Paul's challenge to circumcision and the food laws of Judaism were of the same character. Saying that circumcision did not mark true Jews was *not* an attack on "external" signs and symbols. Paul's challenge to circumcision was a challenge to a particular ordering of the community of God's people. To say the circumcision is nothing is to announce the erection of a new Israel, one in which Jew and Gentile are on an equal footing. It meant that what was once prohibited (Jews eating with Gentiles) became a requirement, and what was once required (Jews refusing to eat with Gentiles) was prohibited. The coming of the Church was a revolution of Judaism's pattern of interdictions and permissions, a change in law, a new cultural order.

The complex of prohibitions is internalized, Rieff claims, under the direction of authoritative cultural guides or "priesthoods": "Priesthoods preside over the origins of a culture and guard its character." Priests shape and guard culture by laying out what may and what may not be done, the interdicts and the remissions. Thus priests stand at the moral boundaries of culture, enforcing those boundaries and ensuring that the culture is perpetuated to another generation by inculcating the culture's "Thou shalt nots."[28]

The writer to the Hebrews would have us know that changes in law are bound up with changes in priesthood, and Rieff's cultural theory suggests a similar pattern: "A crisis in culture occurred whenever old guides were struck dumb, or whenever laities began listening to new guides."[29] For many centuries, Rieff notes, the sociological priesthood of Western civilization was the literal priesthood of the Christian Church, but by Wilde's time churchmen had defaulted in their capacity as authoritative cultural guides. They had fallen silent, and other priesthoods began projecting their ideals onto the "laity." The "post-Christian" West can be seen as the product of the revolutionary changes in law that followed from a revolutionary change of priesthood.

In Rieff's view, no successor priesthood has yet emerged, but Western culture has instead embarked on the unprecedented experiment of forming a non-moral culture, a "culture" lacking religiously grounded prohibitions and refusing to establish a priesthood to guard sacred boundaries. We live in a world celebrated by conservative writers like D'Souza, in which each of us pursues virtue not by external command from some priesthood, but "from within."

Such is, Rieff rightly says, an experiment in "anti-culture."

21

The Church does not agree on, much less enforce, her own "thou shalt nots."

The Church does not even agree that there *are* "thou shalt nots."

The anti-culture has invaded the Church.

22

The specific moral questions confronting the Church today are often the same as those faced by the ancient church. Abortion: Romans exposed infants. Sex: in the imperial period, Rome became famously prodigal and licentious. Homosexuality: many in the ancient world approved certain forms of paedophilia and sodomy as an expression of male love.

What the modern church lacks, however, is consensus about these issues, not to mention enforcement of Christian practices.

Is it any wonder if the Spirit is grieved?

Robert Jenson has pointed out that the permission of abortion is a sign of America's degeneration from justice: "If unborn children are members of the human community, then allowing abortions to be performed on decision of the most interested party is a relapse to pure barbarism."[30]

But we live in an age when even the Church cannot recognize barbarism as barbarism, or name it for what it is.

Is it any wonder if the Spirit is grieved?

Few are willing to admit it, but the sexual abuse scandal in the Catholic church is largely about homosexuality.[31] And it is hardly surprising in a church that has tolerated seminaries that go by nicknames like "Notre Flame" and "Pink Palace," not to mention Jesuit outposts who openly advertise their admiration for gay culture.[32]

Experiments in anti-culture are not cost-free, and Presbyterians, Methodists, Anglicans and other communions that have relaxed Christian prohibitions of sodomy had better brace themselves.

Is it any wonder if the Spirit is grieved?

23

With Rieff, we can well ask, Where are the priests? Who is manning the boundaries?

And the answer is that this dimension of pastoral ministry has all but evaporated. Pastors see themselves as proponents of Christianity, teaching "religious" things or assisting people on their personal spiritual journeys. Pastors have lost any sense that they are overseers of a new city and that they therefore have responsibilities for governance.

In part, this is an effect of the degeneration of the notion of pastoral vocation. If the tension between duty and desire has lost its existential edge in the twenty-first century, it is not because desire has become more vigorous. Instead, the tension has eased because duty has been collapsed into desire. Since Hume, moderns have been forbidden to derive an "ought" from an "is," but it has become second nature to derive an "ought" from a "feels."[33] The consequences lie strewn on the surface of today's social landscape, too obvious to require enumeration.

Historically, a pastoral candidate's desires often had little to do with the Church's call to serve in pastoral office. Far from seeking out positions of leadership, the greatest of the church fathers resisted with all their strength. Augustine had to be dragged into the cathedral for his ordination to the bishopric of Hippo. When he was a deacon, John Chrysostom made a pact with a friend that they would enter the priesthood together, but when the friend went forward John was nowhere to be found. Martin of Tours was carried from his cell and conducted to his ordination under guard. Gregory the Great, so we are told by his earliest biographer, fled from Rome to hide in the woods when rumors began to circulate that he was being considered for bishop. A humble anchorite saw in a vision where Gregory was hiding, and the Romans trooped out to bring him back for ordination. Calvin was persuaded to remain in Geneva only because Farel's warnings made leaving even more terrifying than staying. So common was such resistance to ordination that as late as the nineteenth century the patriarchs-elect of Alexandria were led to their ordination wearing shackles.[34]

In the modern church, calling has been reduced to little more than a strong desire to hold a position of ecclesiastical leadership. The terror of responsibility for the Church described by many of the leading pastoral writers of earlier centuries is seldom expressed during ordination exams.[35] Candidates with even slight reservations about entering the ministry are treated with more than a little suspicion.

This dramatic shift in the Church's understanding of calling is part and parcel of what David F. Wells has identified as the professionalization of the clergy, the reduction of ministry to technical and managerial competence. Pastoral ministry, Wells charges, has been detached from its theological moorings, and has become another career option for the upwardly mobile "helping professional."[36] One might well recoil from a duty imposed by divine vocation; but one aggressively markets oneself for a career. It is no accident that so many pastors disdain the clerical collar, which is, after all, the collar of the slave.

The Church will find herself in a healthier, if more intense and serious, condition when pastoral candidates begin again to appear for their ordination exams wearing chains.

24

For all its animus toward modernity, the Christian Right made one of the most characteristic of modern political beliefs the foundation of its entire agenda: the assumption that the state has jurisdiction of morals. The fact that the name "Moral Majority" was given to what amounted to a political movement betrays this assumption, as does the "social issue agenda" of the Christian Right.

A more radically Christian approach would be for the Church to challenge this assumption by reasserting her own jurisdiction of morals. In the pluralistic West, of course, the Church cannot claim to exercise this function over the whole of society. At least, however, the Church could begin by accepting responsibility for the conduct of her own members. At least, pastors can function as guardian-priests of their own communities.

Revival of the Church's oversight of morals will not occur without conflict. Logically, it is difficult to see why the gay rights agenda should stop at the door of the church; churches have already been sued for violating the civil rights of members censured for practicing homosexual sodomy. If abortion is the absolute constitutional right that some claim, churches that censure abortion providers and advocates will eventually be perceived as fundamentally treasonous.

Without a revival of church discipline, however, the Church will not be constituted as a *polis*. It will remain confined by the heresy of Christianity.

26

Augustine's ecclesiology cuts sharply in two directions. On the one hand, it undermines overly institutional conceptions of the nature of the Church. For Augustine, two communities of believers are not bound together primarily because they are part of the same legal and juridical structure, but because they love one another.

On the other hand, Augustine's ecclesiology makes it simply unthinkable that there could be genuinely Christian communities that did not live in mutual fellowship and love, and this love necessarily is manifested in institutional or governmental cooperation. If Presbyterian church A does not recognize the discipline of Baptist church B, if Methodist church C refuses to have fellowship with Anglican church D, at least one of each pair is schismatic, that is, failing to act out of love for the brethren.

Augustine's ecclesiology finds absolutely no place for competing bodies of Christians, no place for congregations to live side by side without contact or mutual fellowship, no place for refusal of intercommunion among Christian bodies. All these are the practices of schismatics.

27

Jesus prayed that the Church would be one as the Father and Son are one (Jn. 17:22), and Jesus said that the Spirit was the One who testified of the Son who reveals the Father (Jn. 16:25–31).

Schismatic churches lie about the unity of the Father and Son; they dispute the witness of the Spirit. In practice, they are trinitarian heretics.

And we are all schismatics.

Is it any wonder if the Spirit is grieved?

28

Perhaps Ephraim Radner is correct. Perhaps the Spirit has abandoned the Church.[37]

5

For Constantine

1

The mission of the Church can be described as a double movement. On the one hand, the Church is called to withdraw from the world, to be a counterculture, a separate city within the world's cities, challenging and clashing with the world by unapologetically speaking her own language, telling her own stories, enacting her own rites, practicing her own way of life. Though she shares considerable cultural space with the world, the Church is not an institution in the world alongside other institutions. She is an alternative world unto herself, with her roots in heaven, formed by being drawn into the community of Father, Son and Spirit.

The Church is not, however, simply a counterculture. She has been given the subversive mission of converting whatever culture she finds herself in. She works to the end that her language, her rites, and her way of life might become formative for an entire society. She withdraws from the world for the sake of the world. Having been drawn into the communion of the triune God, she participates also in the mission of the triune God.

Christianity cannot carry out this mission, because Christianity proposes only ideas; it does not form a world or a city. Christianity offers the Church only as a new sort of religious association, not as a new, eschatological ordering of human life. So long as Christianity reigns, the Church cannot really be separate; and so

long as Christianity reigns, the Church can never convert anything.

Unless we renounce Christianity, we will have no Christendom.

2

But do we want Christendom? The fact is, Christendom happened. The question is, Was it a big mistake?

3

Some theologians (Stanley Hauerwas, John Howard Yoder, Barry
Harvey, and others) have argued that being against Christianity
entails being against Christendom, and especially against
Constantine. Constantine's conversion, and the consequent
Christianization of the Roman Empire, it is argued, produced
the privatized, spiritualized, intellectualized, depoliticized form
of religion that I have been calling Christianity. If we hope to restore the Church's sense of herself as a separate, holy culture
and distinct civic reality, we must renounce the project of
Christendom.

4

On the contrary, opposition to Christendom arises from adherence to Christianity. Those who are hostile to Christendom are
still in the grip of modernity.

Renouncing Christianity thus entails embracing Christendom.

5

The issue here is not whether the specific shape that Christian civilization took during the Middle Ages is altogether defensible. Everyone agrees that this civilization produced its share of evils and
injustices, which are all the more evil for having been done in the
name of Christ. Everyone agrees that this civilization embodied

the gospel very imperfectly. If Christendom was imperfect, so, naturally, were Constantine, Charlemagne and all the other founders of Christendom. And one imperfection, to be sure, was a tendency to reduce the gospel and Church to Christianity.

Nor is this a question of whether or not the West continues to be Christendom. The modern West is not Christendom in any meaningful sense, and Christians need to learn how to function as the Church without the artificial support of Christian political and cultural systems.[1]

Nor is there any disagreement whether the end of Christendom is a good thing; it is a good thing. Christendom has come under judgment, and every judgment is a reason for hope.

The issue, rather, is whether a Christian civilization that extends beyond the Church is *in itself* a false path. Hauerwas clearly thinks that it is—his book *After Christendom?* bears the subtitle, "How the Church is to behave if freedom, justice, and a Christian nation are bad ideas," and he denies that he "harbor[s] a desire for a 'Christian culture'" or that he longs "for a time when something called 'Christianity' had hegemonic culture and political power."[2] Rodney Clapp is more straightforward: "Constantinianism . . . is a theological and missiological mistake."[3]

The issue is whether the hope of forming Christian culture in the wider society is inherent to the Church's mission, or a deviation from the Church's mission. Should the Christian *ekklesia* want to remake the earthly city in her image?

6

Perhaps we are speaking past one another. Perhaps Clapp's "Constantinianism" is not my "Christendom."

When I use "Christendom," I am referring to the civilization that grew up during the latter patristic and early medieval periods, and which continued, in a very modified form, until the modern era in the West (whenever we wish to date that).

"Christendom" in this sense is "Constantinian" because it assumes and rests upon the fact of Constantine's conversion and
the adoption of the Church as providing the official religion of
the Roman empire.

When I refer to "Constantine," I shall occasionally be refer-
ring to the historical person, the hero of the Battle of Milvian
Bridge. More often, "Constantine" will be short-hand for
"Christian ruler" and "professedly Christian civil order."

7

In the sense I am using the term, Christendom happened. Stark
has pointed out how the Church functioned to renew life in ancient cities. Cities in the early Roman empire were ethnically
and religiously diverse:

> Greco-Roman cities required a constant and substantial stream
> of newcomers simply to maintain their populations. As a result,
> at any given moment a very considerable proportion of the
> population consisted of *recent* newcomers—Greco-Roman cit-
> ies were peopled by strangers. . . . Given the immense cultural
> diversity of the empire, the waves of newcomers to Greco-Ro-
> man cities were of very diverse origins and therefore fractured
> the local culture into numerous ethnic fragments.[4]

As a result, cities were places where enormous strife, chaos,
and crime were facts of life. Stark describes Antioch as

> a city filled with misery, danger, fear, despair, and hatred. A city
> where the average family lived a squalid life in filthy and
> cramped quarters, where at least half of the children died at
> birth or during infancy, and where most of the children who
> lived lost at least one parent before reaching maturity. A city
> filled with hatred and fear rooted in intense ethnic antagonisms
> and exacerbated by a constant stream of strangers. A city so
> lacking in stable networks of attachments that petty incidents
> could prompt mob violence. A city where crime flourished and

the streets were dangerous at night. And, perhaps above all, a city repeatedly smashed by cataclysmic catastrophes: where a resident could literally expect to be homeless from time to time, providing that he or she was among the survivors.[5]

In such a setting, the Church entered as a movement of urban renewal:

> Christianity revitalized life in Greco-Roman cities by providing new norms and new kinds of social relationships able to cope with many urgent urban problems. To cities filled with the homeless and the impoverished, Christianity offered charity as well as hope. To cities filled with newcomers and strangers, Christianity offered an immediate basis for attachments. To cities filled with orphans and widows, Christianity provided a new and expanded sense of family. To cities torn by violent ethnic strife, Christianity offered a new basis for social solidarity. And to cities faced with epidemics, fires, and earthquakes, Christianity offered effective nursing services.[6]

By the Middle Ages, this "urban renewal" program had advanced considerably. Intellectual life was devoted to unraveling the mysteries of God's Word and seeking to name the world, all the world, through the Word. Rules and legal principles drawn from Scripture were worked into the fabric of Western law. The rites of the Church became the festivals of medieval cities; *corpus Christi* is not a feast that Protestants celebrate, but it was a recognizably Christian feast and was a highlight of the year in many places during the late medieval period. Daily lives of Europeans were shaped by the rituals of the Church, from the baptismal cradle through confirmation in puberty through marriage to last rites and the grave. The Church imposed its discipline on warlords and kings, forcing the powers that be to conduct themselves in more humanely, that is, in a more Christlike, fashion.

During the medieval period, the culture of the Church left its mark on the cultural life of Europe in more subtle but no less fundamental ways. George Steiner suggested in his Eliot Lectures that the shared images of Western art and literature were inculcated by Scripture and the liturgies of the Church: "Scriptural and, in a wider sense, religious literacy ran strong, particularly in Protestant lands. The Authorized Version and Luther's Bible carried in their wake a rich tradition of symbolic, allusive, and syntactic awareness. Absorbed in childhood, the Book of Common Prayer, the Lutheran hymnal and psalmody cannot but have marked a broad compass of mental life and their exact, stylized articulateness and music of thought."[7] Literature in the West arose from liturgy.

Even today, in important ways, the modern world is a deviant byproduct, a genetic mutation, of Christendom. Try to imagine the modern novel without the background of the Bible.

8

Rodney Clapp argues that the "Constantinian settlement demands that the Christian faith be privatized and individualized" and that the "Constantinian church is *by definition* reactive and reflexive to the surrounding culture. It completely forgets the church's own culture-forming and sustaining capabilities. It denies any real tension between the church and the world. . . . And it aligns the church with power, against those out of power."[8]

How is it that a church that exercises public authority, that advises kings and emperors, that sponsors the arts, science, and scholarship is accused of promoting a "privatized and individualized" faith? Clapp's assertions are counterintuitive.

But are they wrong?

9

Oliver O'Donovan has argued that Constantinian Christians were not attempting to promote the kingdom of Christ by worldly means. On the contrary, they believed that "those who held power became subject to the rule of Christ."[9] And this is precisely what the "martyr church" was aiming at with its witness unto death: "This was the logical conclusion of their confidence in mission, the confirmation of what they had always predicted. The kings of the earth had come to bow before the throne of Christ, and the empire they had served had lost its most powerful agents."[10] Christendom meant not "the church's seizing alien power" but "alien power's becoming attentive to the church."[11]

Invoking the martyrs without also invoking this hope is an insult to the memory of the martyrs.

10

John Howard Yoder has described the effects of Constantine's conversion by pointing to the ecclesiological, eschatological, and metaphysical results of that conversion.[12]

By filling the Church with nominal believers, Constantinianism encouraged a change in the meaning of the word *Christian* and in the understanding of the Church. Earlier, a Christian was a baptized person who had adopted the way of life demanded by Jesus, but after Constantine, the word "could no longer be identified with baptism and church membership, since many who are 'Christian' in that sense had not themselves chosen to follow Christ." The fact that many within the Church did not meet the early Christian definition of "Christian" led to the idea of an invisible church: "The class of *true* Christians continues to be a minority," but now the minority was a "church within a church," rather than a minority within the Roman empire. Under the Constantinian settlement, the nature of mission changed. It no longer involved "calling one's hearers to faith in Jesus Christ as Lord" but instead "became identical with the expansion of Rome's sway." Church leaders assumed the role of "chaplains" to political powers, rather than acting as leaders of an alternative political power.

Constantinianism encouraged a strongly "realized" eschatology, viewing the present Roman empire as a historical embodiment of the kingdom of God: "The concept of millennium was soon pulled back from the future (whether distant or imminent) into the present." Providence, at the same time, came to be understood as something empirically evident "in the person of the Christian ruler of the world." Thus, the Roman state (and later, the nation-states of the early modern era) came to be seen as the carriers of history. History no longer centered on the people of God, but on kings, nobles, and potentates.

Yoder summarizes the ecclesiological and eschatological results in a much-quoted formula:

> Before Constantine, one knew as a fact of everyday experience that there was a believing Christian community but one had to "take it on faith" that God was governing history. After Constantine, one had to believe without seeing that there was a community of believers, within the larger nominally Christian mass, but one knew for a fact that God was in control of history.

As Yoder reads the early history of the Church, the teachings of Jesus, especially the sermon on the Mount, formed the content of ethical instruction for every Christian, whatever their particular business in life. When Roman and Germanic civilizations were "baptized," diverse callings came to be seen as "natural" features of economic and social life, and their ethical contours were seen as inherent in the calling itself. A Christian trader was no longer expected to follow Jesus' teachings; he was expected to conform to the natural laws of trade. A Christian ruler was not expected to use power in accord with Jesus' teachings; he was expected to exercise dominion just like any other ruler would. Only those who had specifically "religious" vocations—monks and priests—were expected to conform to Jesus' teachings. Thus, Constantinianism introduced a dualism into the Church's life between "religious" and "non-religious" members. By granting some measure of autonomy to "non-religious" callings, Constantinianism opened up a window of opportunity for the introduction of "secularism," and, simultaneously, for Christianity.

In this way, Constantinianism encouraged the development of a dualistic metaphysics. While Neoplatonism was the main philosophical source, philosophy alone cannot explain the dominance of dualistic modes of thought within the Church: "Naming its source does not explain its success." Rather, dualism triumphed because it cohered with the actual life and practices of the Church, providing metaphysical grounding for Constantinian ecclesial and social life:

> The church we see is not the believing community; the visible/ invisible duality names, and thereby justifies, the tension. The dominant ethic is different from the New Testament in content (Lordship is glorified rather than servanthood) as in source (reason and the "orders of creation" are normative, rather than the particularity of Jesus' and the apostles' guidance). What could be easier than to reserve the ethics of love for the inward or for the personal, while the ethics of power are for the outward world of structures? Interiorization and individualization, like the developments of the special worlds of cult and mediation, were not purely philosophical invasions which took over because they were intellectually convincing. They did so also because they were functional. They explained and justified the growing distance from Jesus and his replacement by other authorities and another political vision other than that of the kingdom of God.

For Yoder, as for Clapp (who draws on Yoder), Constantinianism produced Christianity.

11

Even if Yoder's historical claims are entirely justified (and many of them are), he has not proven that "Christendom" or "Christian civilization" *as such* was a mistake. He concedes as

much in an illuminating meditation on the question, What if
Constantine had been more faithful?

> One could say that Caesar would be just as free as anyone else
> to take risks in faith. In fact, in an authentically imperial society
> . . . Caesar would be perfectly free (for a while) to bring to
> bear upon the exercise of his office the ordinary meaning of
> Christian faith. It might happen that the result would be that his
> enemies would triumph over him, but that often happens to
> rulers anyway. It might happen that he would have to suffer, or
> not stay in office all his life, but that too often happens to rulers
> anyway, and it is something that Christians are supposed to be
> ready for. It might happen that he would be killed—but most
> Caesars are killed anyway. It might happen that some of his fol-
> lowers would have to suffer. But emperors and kings are accus-
> tomed to asking people to suffer for them. Especially if the
> view were still authentically alive, which the earlier Christians
> undeniably had held to and which the theologians of the age of
> Constantine were still repeating, that God blesses those who
> serve him, it might also have been possible that, together with
> all the risks just described, most of which a ruler accepts any-
> way, there could have been in some times and in some places
> the possibility that good could be done, that creative social al-
> ternatives could be discovered, that problems could be solved,
> enemies loved and justice fostered.[13]

Denying the possibility of such an outcome, Yoder suggests, is
a sign of "systematic pessimism" that is incompatible with "the
rhetoric of Christian belief in providence."

Yet this means that the evils of "Constantinianism" were his-
torical accidents, not inevitable results of the conversion of the
Roman empire. Yoder does not see that the hypothetical "faithful
Constantine" fundamentally challenges his case against
Constantinianism.

12

Yoder, the Mennonite theologian, was an apologist for the idea of Christendom.

13

Some of Yoder's arguments are seriously flawed.

For instance, does the New Testament highlight the Sermon on the Mount, or the teaching of Jesus in general, as the Alpha and Omega of Christian ethics?

Historically, this is a dubious claim. The teaching of Jesus was an intervention in the history of Israel, which was a history of debate and dialogue concerning the demands of Torah. Jesus did not start *de novo*, propounding a completely new Torah; instead, He propounded a reading of Torah.

And Torah contains guidelines for the godly use of power that are not contradicted by Jesus' teachings on Torah.

14

Yet, my argument is not so much against Yoder himself as against the "systematic pessimism" that he identifies and does not altogether escape. Yoder's faithful Constantine would have produced a very different world from the one the real Constantine produced, and Yoder's vision of a Christian politics differs radically from mine (for starters, he was a pacifist, and I am not). But Yoder seems to agree that a Christian politics, outside the polity of the Church, is a real-world possibility. Those who deny this possibility, the pessimists, have assumed Christianity, and therefore are still modernists, despite their fulminations against modernity.

Consider: Yoder says, "If *kenosis* is the shape of God's own self-sending, then any strategy of Lordship, like that of the kings of this world, is not only a strategic mistake likely to backfire but a denial of gospel substance."[14] If we leave things here (which Yoder himself does not quite do), we are left with a dilemma and even heresy.

Heresy first: Yoder assumes that "Lordship" always and everywhere must be the Lordship of the "kings of this world." This cannot be the case, for the ultimate Lordship is exercised, as Yoder would have remembered if he had extended his quotation a few verses further in Philippians 2, precisely by the self-emptying Son. Equating "Lordship" with "worldly Lordship" is Christological (and theological) heresy. Who *is* Lord, anyway?

Second, the dilemma, unfolded in several stages: To say that Lordship always and everywhere is worldly is to say that the governance of cities and nations and empires is impervious to the influence of the gospel. Worldly politics is the only game *currently* in town; even worse, it is the only *possible* game in town.

To say that worldly politics is the only game in town is to suggest that the political world is autonomous and secular—fundamentally, necessarily, and unchangeably so. This is modernism, and, on Yoder's terms, "Constantinian." This rests on the assumption that power cannot be exercised in a Christlike fashion, and that is precisely the assumption of the most naive defenders of Constantine—namely, that Constantine's unchristian political actions are to be excused because he is a politician, and everyone knows that politicians are above the rules that govern the rest of us. Rejecting Constantine lands the pessimist, paradoxically, among the "Constantinians."

Finally, the corollary is that the Church does not really have much to say to worldly powers, at least nothing that can be effective. The Church might have some effective word for its members, some pious advice for the private life of the ruler, but has no words of power to speak to power. This is Christianity, the assumption that the Bible addresses only the private and personal. Rejection of "Constantinian" privatization lands the pessimists, paradoxically, with the privatizers.

In the end, this systematic pessimism is simply a disbelief that the gospel describes the way things really are. For if the gospel describes the way things really are, it describes the way politics really is, and that should make it clear politics is not the autonomous secular sphere imagined by modern politicians. It should make clear that politics can be shaped to the gospel and that the kingdoms of this world have and will, more and more, become the kingdoms of our Lord and of His Christ.

15

Once there was a prophet named Stanley. The prophet Stanley was a bold and faithful man who stood with granite face against the powers of the age.

"You cannot do that s—t," he would say, as he stood before the king. "You are going to end up in f——g h—l, and your people are going to hate you."

One day, the king began to listen and to see the wisdom of Stanley's words. When Stanley told him that the weak must be protected from the vicious strong, the king took steps to protect the weak. When Stanley told him that Jesus was Lord, the king bowed his knee. When Stanley told him that religious freedom is a subtle temptation, the king took heed.

And the king made a proclamation, that all in his kingdom should wear sackcloth and ashes and repent of their sins, even to the least beast of burden.

And Stanley went out from the city and made a shelter and sat under it and refused to speak again to the king.

And Stanley said, "Lord, please take my life from me, for death is better to me than life. I am a d—n prophet, not a f——g chaplain."

And the Lord said, "Do you have good reason to be angry?"

As for the king, he was greatly confounded and confused, and knew not what to do; for he had done all that Stanley had asked.

This parable ends with questions, not a moral: Will the king always refuse to listen? Says who? And, when the king begins to listen, must the Church fall silent, so as to avoid becoming a chaplain? To keep her integrity, must the Church *refuse* to succeed?

16

So long as the Church preaches the gospel and functions as a properly "political" reality, a polity of her own, the kings of the earth have a problem on their hands. Some Haman will notice that there is a people in the empire who do not live according to the laws of the Medes, and reports will come from the colonies that there are men attacking the decrees of Caesar and proclaiming another King. As soon as the Church appears, it becomes clear to any alert politician that worldly politics is no longer the only game in town. The introduction of the Church into *any* city means that the city has a challenger within its walls. This *necessarily* forces political change, ultimately of constitutional dimensions.

Suppose the king recognizes the Church as a counterweight to his own authority, or even, however grudgingly, as a prophetic voice. In that case, we are dashing off to Christendom, even if we run most of the way alongside Yoder and Hauerwas.

Suppose the king tries to suppress the Church legally or through extralegal violence. In that case, a clash is unavoidable, one that kings have had difficulty winning. Besides, suppressing the Church is itself a constitutional decision, a decision that the king will *not* accept the Church as a counter-kingdom alongside his own kingdom. That is a statement about the character of the political order, which clarifies its claim to monopoly of authority and which sounds like a claim to a monopoly of worship. Should the king suppress the Church, he shows his true colors, and it becomes obvious that his regime is implicitly totalitarian.

Suppose the king is a liberal who tries to police the boundaries of the Church, telling the Church where it can and cannot speak, what it can and cannot do. In that case too, a clash is inevitable and, again, kings have a hard time winning such battles. Besides, once the king decides to police the boundaries of the Church, he is again making claims of a constitutional order about the extent of his power.

On the other hand, if the Church appears preaching Christianity, the king is entirely capable of stealing the rhetoric and story and ideas of the Church to buttress his power. Every Constantine can find an amateur Eusebius who will use numerology to prove that his kingdom is the fulfillment of Israel's prophetic hope. Or, political powers may simply force Christianity into the private sphere—shoving ideas back into the brain and Christianity back into the churches. Churches in the grip of Christianity will hardly blink when the liberal king tells them that they have to confine themselves to thinking pious thoughts.

17

There is an incoherence in the work of Hauerwas, Yoder, and others who would defend the Church as *polis* but attack the idea of a Christian civilization and a Christian political order.

Ultimately, hostility to Christendom is hostility to social consensus, but this hostility is also an attack on the Church. As O'Donovan has argued, modern suspicion about the dangers of consensus as the basis for government (the fear that consensus is coercive) are based on "a radical suspicion of society as such and the agreements that constitute it." But a suspicion about "society as such" and the inherently "coercive" nature of consensus also rules out the possibility of the Church: "If any social agreement is potentially coercive and to be justified only by the needs of the civil order, then the agreements which constitute the church, with which many disagree, are coercive and unjustifiably so."[15]

This is quite clearly a variety of hyperliberalism. And it is fully consonant with the heresy of Christianity, for it implies that the Church cannot be a *polity* organized by a common story, sharing one faith, one hope, submitting to one Lord.

Even if exception is made for the Church, opposition to consensus implies that societies outside the Church cannot have an overarching narrative except through coercion. But that implies, in turn, that worldly society is impervious to the gospel, that it is unchangeably and permanently secular. As O'Donovan says,

Christendom ought to be the kind of storied community [narrative theologians such as Hauerwas] aim to celebrate. Of course, they criticise it not for having a story but for having the wrong story, a story made up of the praise of coercion; but that is precisely where they succumb to the liberal thesis. The storytellers of Christendom do not celebrate coercion; they celebrate the power of God to humble the haughty ones of the earth and to harness them to the purposes of peace. In resolving to reconstruct the self-storying of Christendom the narrativists have simply followed the principle proposed by their adversaries: social doctrine of whatever kind is coercive; those who claim a social identity in terms of unnecessary belief do violence to those who do not share it.[16]

18

So: Is Stanley too among the liberals?

19

Opposition to Christendom often takes the form, positively, of a "voluntary" conception of the Church. But then, what has happened to the vision of the Church as a counter-*polis*? O'Donovan asks, "Is Yoder, in the name of non-conformity, not championing a great conformism, lining the church up with the sports clubs, friendly societies, colleges, symphony subscription-guilds, political parties and so on, just to prove that the church offers late-modern order no serious threat?"[17]

Reducing the Church in this way is a capitulation to modernity and is Christianity in the purest form.

20

To rephrase: Is Yoder too among the liberals?

21

Infant baptism is the nub of the issue: Baptist and Anabaptist advocates of the "voluntary church" are the ones whose baptismal theology is a theology of conformity with the values of the world—because Baptist theology is Christianity.

22

Dieter Georgi is exactly right in his description of the implications of calling the Christian community *ekklesia*:

> Paul chose [*ekklesia*] to indicate that the assembly of those who followed Jesus, the assembly called together in a particular city in the name of the biblical God, was in competition with the local political assembly of the citizenry, the official *ekklesia*. The world is meant to hear the claim that the congregation of Jesus, gathered in the name of the God of the Bible, is where the interests of the city in question truly find expression.[18]

Had the apostles adopted the term "synagogue" to describe their assemblies, the note of opposition and confrontation of Greco-Roman politics would have been muffled.

Again, there is an incoherence at the heart of the work of Yoder, Hauerwas, and their followers: the Church as *ekklesia* is, precisely because it is *ekklesia*, making a claim to governance of the city. Why, after all, set up an *ekklesia* unless you're planning to run a city?

23

When the Church arrives, there will be clashes that force constitutional changes, unless, as Robert Jenson has said in a different context, we have forgotten ourselves.

Too often we have done precisely that.

23

Suppose we don't forget ourselves, and the powers attack us. What then?

The book of Revelation describes a conflict of cities. The city of God, which is the bride that comes from heaven, stands against an alliance of Jerusalem and Rome.[19] The "great city" that falls in Revelation 17–18 is identified in 11:8 as "the great city, where the Lord was crucified." From that point on, there are numerous references to the "great city" (16:19; 17:18; 18:10, 16, 18), all of which refer to the "circumcision party" spread throughout the Mediterranean world. Even the name "Babylon" suggests that the city is a false bride, a false church, a false "gate of heaven," as Babel pretended to be. But Jerusalem, the harlot, rides upon a great beast with seven heads and ten horns, and this image shows Jerusalem and Judaism supported by the power of the Roman empire (17:1–18). Though initially allied, the beast and the harlot have a falling out, and the beast begins to hate the harlot and seeks to destroy her (17:16).

Earlier, John described a great tribulation, organized by the serpent who employs the combined forces of the two beasts, the sea beast and land beast. Again, these are images of Rome and Jerusalem, allied with Satan and with one another against the Church. At the end of chapter 14, there is a harvest scene in which one like the Son of Man stretches out His scythe to gather from the grapevines and wheat fields (14:14–18). As in the gospels, the harvest scene does not describe a judgment but a gathering, and it is the saints, those who partake of bread and wine (we are what we eat), who are being gathered. Though the beasts intend to destroy the people of the table, in fact it is the Son of Man who is gathering them to Himself, so that they may have "rest from their labors" (14:13).

Once the harvest is complete, the clusters of grapes are thrown "into the great wine press of the wrath of God," which is "trodden outside the city, and blood came out from the wine press, up to the horses' bridles, for a distance of two hundred miles" (14:19b–20). Like the master they served, the saints shed their blood "outside the camp," and their blood fills the land (cf. Heb. 13:12–14).

John's vision is then directed to heaven, where He sees before the throne of God seven angels with "golden bowls full of the wrath of God" (15:2,7), which they pour out on the earth (16:1–21). In context, the "wrath of God" that the angels pour out came from the "wine press of the wrath of God" in which the grapes were pressed. Angels are pouring out the blood of the saints—seven times—on the earth and the city, with the result that the city is cast down, burned, destroyed.

What happens if the earthly city should resist the heavenly city? If the resistance is to the point of shedding blood, then the blood of the martyrs will call from the ground for vengeance. And the God of vengeance will shine forth and render a reward to the proud.

The mere presence of the Church means the end to "business as usual" in the earthly city. Always and forever, an end to business as usual.

24

O'Donovan has pointed out, in a critique of Hauerwas, that the idea of a permanent martyr church misses one of the key elements of the martyrs' vision: vindication. A church forever martyred without relief is a cross without a resurrection.

Ultimately, Hauerwas's oversight is one of theology proper: God is not the God of the dead, or of the dying; He is God of the living, of the living again. As Jenson says, he is the God who is faithful to death, and then "yet again faithful."

Therefore: no cross without resurrection, no martyrdom without vindication, no exile without return, no (martyr) church without (converted) Constantine. Or God is not God.

And vice versa as well: no resurrection without the cross, no vindication without martyrdom. The Church can gain victory only on the other side of the cross. She finds her way to the city center by first being led to the gibbet outside the city walls.

Rene Girard is right in this case at least: the scapegoat driven
from the city is in fact the savior, who returns to inhabit the
temple in the *agora*.

Without the shedding of blood there is no new city.

25

"Forsake" is a key word in Jeremiah's indictment of Judah: the
people have forsaken the Lord and gone after other gods (1:16;
2:13), and Judah has become like her sister Israel, a faithless
bride, a prostitute who lies with foreign men under every green
tree. Because Judah has forsaken her Lord, He is going to forsake her, and even forsake His temple (12:7). He will leave the
people unprotected, vulnerable to the judgments of sword, fam-
ine, and pestilence. Judah will be removed from the land of
promise and taken into exile in a strange land. Judah has broken
the marriage covenant, and Jeremiah is assigned to deliver the
writ of divorce against her.

Dark and gloomy as Jeremiah's message is, it is ultimately a
message of hope. In the chapters known as Jeremiah's "little
book of comfort" (chaps. 30–33), the prophet speaks of the
guideposts that mark out the way of return (30:21) and claims
that the bride that returns will be a virgin, no longer a prostitute. Songs of worship will again be heard; cities and their com-
merce will be restored, as will the farmer and his flock (vv.
23–26). The land will no longer be desolate, formless and void,
decreated under the judgment of God. Rather, the Lord will sow
it with man and beast, planting his vine in the land and building
Israel as His house (31:27–28).

Though this promise of a new covenant was ultimately fulfilled in Jesus, the Jews who returned to the land after the exile
also saw the first fulfillment of these promises. By the time we
get to the New Testament, the Word of the Lord has gone forth
from Zion, such that there are men from "every tribe under
heaven" in Jerusalem to hear Peter's sermon at Pentecost, and

Paul can find flourishing synagogues throughout Asia Minor, consisting of both Jews and converted Gentiles.

After exile came resurrection. Exile was a judgment, but God judged His Church in order to purge and strengthen her. Exile was a death, but God kills in order to raise up again.

26

The modern church is in exile; we have chosen exile, and the Lord has delivered us to our desires. But we do not worship the God of permanent exile. We worship the God of exodus.

He calls us to faith, and that means renouncing Christianity and all its works and all its pomp. It means clinging to the gospel, believing the gospel, preaching the gospel, living the gospel as the Church, even to the shedding of blood.

27

Perhaps Ephraim Radner is correct. Perhaps the Spirit has abandoned the Church.

But when He abandons Jerusalem, He always reappears with the exiles in Babylon (Ezek. 8–11); when He leaves the synagogue behind, He's found in the Church. He always returns, somewhere. He always returns.

When He does, and where He does, the wilderness blossoms like a rose, parched land flows with springs, and dry bones come to life.

For God is not a God of the dead, but of the living—the God of the living again.

NOTES FOR CHAPTER 1

1. Charles Taylor's definition of secular modernity is handy: "Modernity is secular, not in the frequent, rather loose sense of the word, where it designates the absence of religion, but rather in the fact that religion occupies a different place, compatible with the sense that all social action takes place in profane time." Taylor is delighted with this: "We're living in the best political order yet achieved in human history." I am not; if all social action takes place in "profane time," then the Church's actions do not qualify as social actions. These quotations are from an interview with Taylor by Bruce Ellis Benson, "What it Means to Be Secular," *Books & Culture* 8 (July/August 2002): 37.

2. Wayne A. Meeks, *The First Urban Christians: The Social World of the Apostle Paul* (New Haven: Yale, 1983), 152–153.

3. Ibid.,36.

4. See my brief critique of anti-supercessionist theologian R. Kendall Soulen in *A House for My Name: A Survey of the Old Testament* (Moscow, Idaho: Canon, 2000), 21–26.

5. This reflects Oliver O'Donovan's careful description of the Church's political character: "Describing the church as a political society means to say that it is brought into being and held in being, not by a special function it has to fulfill [as a private club might have—PJL], but by a government that it obeys in everything. It is ruled and authorized by the ascended Christ alone and supremely; it therefore has its own authority; and it is not answerable to any other authority that may subsume it" (*The Desire of Nations: Rediscovering the Roots of Political Theology* [Cambridge: Cambridge University Press, 1996], 159). I register some disagreement with O'Donovan's claim that we call the Church a political society "analogously" and that she "is not another member of the category that might be displayed, say, by reading a list of the nation-states of the United Nations Organization" (ibid.). The latter point is quite true, but not because the Church is only "analogously" political; rather, it is true because the Church is a United Nations Organization. Put differently, more Augustinianly, the Church is the *true* polity or commonwealth, and the phrase "political society" is analogously applied to other political communities.

6. For Aristotle, the difference between *oikos* and *polis* was crucial to the structure of the city, since a city was defined as an association of households. This dualism is seen in the distribution of sexual roles: women were confined to the *oikos* and had no rights as citizens of the *polis*. For the New Testament, the Church is both city and household, and thereby breaks down this structural principle of ancient society. Strikingly and predictably, men *and* women are found in her assemblies and share full rights as citizens. See Reinhard Hutter, "The Church as Public: Dogma, Practice, and the Holy Spirit," *Pro Ecclesia* 3, no. 3 (1994), esp. 352–354. Hutter's point should be qualified by the fact that Aristotle uses *polis* in different senses at various points in the *Politics*. See Hansen in Wallace.

7. I owe the idea that *koinonia* in Acts 2 refers to alms to a lecture given by Rev. Wes Baker at the Pre-GA Conference on Reformed Liturgy, Birmingham, Alabama, June 2002.

8. Gerald F. Hawthorne, *Philippians* (Word Biblical Commentary; Waco: Word, 1983), xxxii–xxxvi.

9. Stanley K. Stowers, "Friends and Enemies in the Politics of Heaven: Reading Theology in Philippians," in Jouette M. Bassler, ed., *Pauline Theology, Volume I: Thessalonians, Philippians, Galatians, Philemon* (Minneapolis: Fortress, 1991), 105–121. Much of the information in the following paragraphs is from Stowers, though he does not draw the particular conclusions I do.

10. Further, Scripture often refers to "friends" of the king, who serve as counsellors and assistants to a ruler. Abraham was a friend of God, and that means that Yahweh consults him when he plans to destroy Sodom (Gen. 18). David's administration of Israel included the position of "king's friend" (2 Sam. 15:37; 16:16). Jesus designated his disciples as "friends" in this same sense; as His friends, He would share all His plans with them and they would assist Him in His rule (John 15:15). From this larger perspective, then, it is also clear that a "society of friends" is not, biblically speaking, a private organization.

11. My exposition of chapter 3 follows that of N. T. Wright, "Paul's Gospel and Caesar's Empire," in Richard A. Horsley, ed., *Paul and Politics: Essays in Honor of Krister Stendahl* (Harrisburg, Penn.: Trinity Press International, 2000), 173–181.

12. See Dieter Georgi, *Theocracy in Paul's Praxis and Theology* (Minneapolis: Fortress, 1991), 72, who claims that Paul deliberately suppressed political themes in his prison correspondence.

13. Josephus used *ekklesia* to refer both to Israel and the Greco-Roman political institution. See Howard-Brook, *The Church Before Christianity* (Maryknoll: Orbis Books, 2001), 30, 34.

14. This from R. Joseph Hoffmann's general introduction to Celsus, *On the True Doctrine: A Discourse Against Christians* (Oxford: Oxford UP, 1987).

15. Quoted in Wayne A. Meeks, *The Origins of Christian Morality: The First Two Centuries* (New Haven: Yale, 1993), 8–9.

16. See Ekkehard W. Stegemann and Wolfgang Stegemann, *The Jesus Movement: A Social History of Its First Century* (Minneapolis: Fortress, 1999), 273–274.

17. John Tomlinson, *Globalization and Culture* (Chicago: University of Chicago Press, 1999); Roland Robertson, "Globalization and the Future of 'Traditional Religion,'" in *Religion and the Powers of the Common Life*, vol. 1 of *God and Globalization*, ed.

Max L. Stackhouse and Peter J. Paris (Harrisburg, Penn.: Trinity Press International, 2000), 53–68; Samuel P. Huntington, *The Clash of Civilizations and the Remaking of World Order* (New York: Touchstone, 1997), esp. chapter 3.

18. One of the best known treatments is the "McDonaldization" thesis propounded by George Ritzer. Ritzer is referring to the global spread of American patterns of consumption, of which McDonald's provides a key, symbolic example. See, for example, Ritzer, *Explorations in the Sociology of Consumption: Fast Food, Credit Cards and Casinos* (London: SAGE, 2001). For a vivid treatment of globalization, which is also careful in specifying how the world is and is not becoming a global culture, see Thomas L. Friedman, *The Lexus and the Olive Tree: Understanding Globalization* (New York: Farrar Straus Giroux, 1999).

19. Wills's article is analyzed in Stanley Hauerwas, *In Good Company: The Church as Polis* (Notre Dame: University of Notre Dame Press, 1995), 199–202. Virtually the same view of "religion and government" may be found in another conservative writer, Dinesh D'Souza, *What's So Great About America* (Washington, D. C.: Regnery, 2002), 89–94. One is left aghast that Christians continue to be attracted to American conservatism. It is another effect of Christianity, under whose influence Christians forget or never learn that they have a politics of their own and have no need of borrowing from either right or left.

20. For an excellent alternative account, see William Cavanagh, "'A Fire Strong Enough to Consume the House': The Wars of Religion and the Rise of the State," *Modern Theology* 11 (1995): 397–420. Cavanagh claims that the opposing armies in the "religious wars" did not line up along confessional lines (Catholics often fought with Protestants against other Catholics, etc.), and that the result of these wars was not so much to separate "religion" from "politics" as to create the category of "religion" as a realm of life that could be isolated and removed from political life.

21. I owe this remark to my friend Clive Brown, of London.

22. See *No Place for Truth: Or, Whatever Happened to Evangelical Theology?* (Grand Rapids: Eerdmans, 1993).

23. This paragraph summarizes the detailed arguments of John Milbank, *Theology and Social Theory*, chapters 3–5. It is not surprising that Berger ends up endorsing Schleiermacher's view of religion as the most adequate response to modernity; Berger begins with liberal Protestant assumptions and concludes with an endorsement of the same. This would not be a serious problem were Berger willing to abandon the claim that his sociology is "scientific."

24. George Weigel, *Soul of the World: Notes on the Future of Public Catholicism* (Washington, D.C.: Ethics and Public Policy Center, 1996), 38.

25. For further theological critique of the idea of "civil society," see Arne Rasmusson, *The Church as Polis: From Political Theology to Theological Politics as Exemplified by Jurgen Moltmann and Stanley Hauerwas* (Notre Dame: University of Notre Dame Press, 1995), 360–367.

NOTES FOR CHAPTER 2

1. Evangelical theologian Millard J. Erickson makes this explicit: "Doctrine deals with general or timeless truths about God and the rest of reality" (*Introducing*

Christian Doctrine, 2d ed., ed. by L. Arnold Hustad [Grand Rapids: Baker, 2001], 16).

2. Quoted in Merold Westphal, *Overcoming Onto-Theology: Toward a Postmodern Christian Faith* (New York: Fordham UP, 2001), 16. In spite of Westphal's spirited defense of Heidegger, I remain convinced that Heidegger is fully modern, still confining theology to an "ontic" status that can be corrected by the science of being, philosophy.

3. I am echoing the well-known claims of George Lindbeck's *The Nature of Doctrine*. Christian doctrine, however, is not *only* a matter of regulating the cultural-linguistic practice of the Church; that is one element, but the creeds also claim to be speaking about what is so, and the cultural-linguistic practice of the Church should be regulated by what is so. Lindbeck's definition of the purpose of doctrine does, however, have the salutary effect of eliminating any separation of theory and application.

4. Quoted in Westphal, *Overcoming Onto-theology*, 11–12.

5. Some of the church fathers, and many more modern theologians, failed to note that the "natural" philosophers were in fact "civic." Plato was *not* doing epistemology; fundamentally, he was doing ethics and politics. One of Plato's most thorough discussions of knowledge, after all, comes in the *Republic*, as part of an exploration of the qualifications for the philosophers who will rule the ideal commonwealth. Theologians who play on the field marked off by philosophers should at least note how the philosophers have marked the field.

6. This quotation is from an excerpt of Robertson Smith's *Lectures on the Religion of the Semites*, found in Robert A. Segal, ed., *The Myth and Ritual Theory* (Oxford: Blackwell, 1998), 27–28.

7. On the connections between poetry and politics, see Mark Munn, *The School of History: Athens in the Age of Socrates* (Berkeley: University of California Press, 2000), 34–36.

8. This latter example is drawn from Simon Price, *Religions of the Ancient Greeks*, Key Themes in Ancient History (Cambridge: Cambridge UP, 1999), 22.

9. It must be emphasized here that I am not using "myth" in the popular sense, in which it is contrasted to "truth." Rather, "myth" here refers to an account of a culture's relation to God (or the gods), which often takes the form of an account of the origins of the society. In this sense, myths may be historically true or not. C. S. Lewis used the term in a similar way when he talked about Christianity as "true myth," though I am highlighting the sociological dimensions of myth more than Lewis.

10. For a rich account of the place of myth in classic Greek life, see Richard Buxton, *Imaginary Greece: The Contexts of Mythology* (Cambridge: Cambridge UP, 1994).

11. N. T. Wright, *Jesus and the Victory of God* (London: SPCK, 1996); see also Marcus Borg, *Conflict, Holiness and Politics in the Teaching of Jesus* and *Jesus: A New Vision* (London: SPCK, 1994).

12. N. T. Wright makes this point in a paper available at <http://www.northpark.edu/sem/exauditu/papers/wright.html>.

13. (Trans. Helen Lane; New York: Farrar Straus Giroux, 1989).

14. A useful collection of work in this area, with preference to philosophical and theological perspectives, is Stanley Hauerwas and L. Gregory Jones, eds., *Why Narrative? Readings in Narrative Theology* (Eugene, Ore.: Wipf & Stock, 1997).

15. Wayne Booth describes the effect that reading about Joyce's Stephen Daedalus had on him as a young reader in his *In Good Company*, one of the most purely pleasurable books I have ever encountered.

16. Martin P. Nilsson, *A History of Greek Religion* (trans. F. J. Fielden; Oxford: Clarendon, 1925), 237.

17. This is the characterization offered by Ethelbert Stauffer, *Christ and the Caesars* (trans. K. and R. Gregor Smith; Philadelphia: Westminster, 1955), 91–101.

18. Dieter Georgi, "Who Is the True Prophet?" in Richard A. Horsley, *Paul and Empire: Religion and Power in Roman Imperial Society* (Harrisburg, Penn.: Trinity Press International, 1997), 41. The quotations from Ovid and Horace in this paragraph also come from Georgi's article.

19. Scholars estimate that Romans crucified tens of thousands of Jews during the first century. In 4 B.C., one rebellion was put down with the crucifixion of 2000 rebels, and around A.D. 50, Felix crucified so many *lestai* (brigands) that Josephus says they were uncountable. Florus, his successor, plundered the temple, provoking rebellion, and this was suppressed by mass crucifixions. During the siege of Jerusalem, Titus crucified as many as 500 per day so that Josephus said that "there was not room enough for the crosses" outside the city walls. See Martin Hengel, *Crucifixion* (Philadelphia: Fortress, 1977); Neil Elliott, "The Anti-Imperial Message of the Cross," in Horsley, ed., *Paul and Empire*, 167–183.

20. N. T. Wright, *Colossians and Philemon*, Tyndale New Testament Commentaries (Grand Rapids: Eerdmans, 1986), 114–118.

21. *Whose Justice? Which Rationality?* (Notre Dame: University of Notre Dame Press, 1988), chap. 17.

22. The myth of liberal democracy is embodied in law, textbooks and other elements of the education curriculum, in political rhetoric and institutions, in holidays, national symbols and anthems, and the national "shrines" that dominate Washington, D. C. There can hardly be a more dramatic expression of this philosophy than the Supreme Court decision, *Casey v. Planned Parenthood*, which based abortion rights in the Fourteenth Amendment's liberty clause. In the decision Justices Souter, O'Connor, and Kennedy agreed that "At the heart of liberty is the right to define one's own concept of existence, of meaning, the universe, and of the mystery of human life." As Gerard Bradley commented at the time, Americans have a constitutional right to "define our own moral universe."

23. William Carroll Bark, *Origins of the Medieval World* (Stanford: Stanford UP, 1958).

24. Though it does not belong in the Lord's Day worship, it is exceedingly important for Christians to recover some sense of the sweep of church history. Not only the Bible but the history of the Church must be embraced as our history. Protestants have all too often acted as if the Church sprang into being on October 31, 1517, with Luther's 95 Theses, and Americans tend to operate with an even

more radically foreshortened sense of history, as if the Framer's claim to be founding a *novus ordo saeclorum* were literally true. As a result, American churches at best celebrate the exploits of Reformation heroes, at worst limit their pantheon to American heroes, redesigned as evangelical Christians. Restoring the Christian story requires giving an important place in Christian consciousness to the heroes of the whole Church—not just Luther but Stephen Langton, not just Calvin but also Chrysostom, not only Bucer but also Boniface and Becket. A wonderful beginning has been made by Richard Hannula in his *Trial and Triumph: Stories from Church History* (Moscow, Idaho: Canon, 1999).

25. (Grand Rapids: Eerdmans, 1992).

26. *Desire of Nations*, 49.

27. How can we learn the Psalms? First, it is best to sing through the entire Psalm, rather than a portion, and it is preferable to chant the actual text of the Psalm rather than a versified Psalm. Second, several suggestions might be made about how to implement the learning of Psalms: declare a moratorium on singing hymns until we have learned all 150 Psalms; introduce one or two Psalms a month, singing them every Sunday, perhaps one in the morning service and one in the evening; use Sunday School time to learn Psalms; teach children Psalms in their Sunday School classes; spend time in school, college, or seminary chapel services learning the Psalms. At Christ Church in Moscow, we have an hour-long Psalm sing once a month on a Sunday evening. However it is done, it must be done.

NOTES FOR CHAPTER 3

1. Mary Douglas, *Natural Symbols: Explorations in Cosmology* (New York: Pantheon, 1973), 1.

2. Quoted in Marshall Berman, *All That Is Solid Melts Into Air: The Experience of Modernity* (New York: Penguin, [1982] 1988), 317.

3. Jane Jacobs, *Death and Life of Great American Cities* (New York: Random House, 1961).

4. David Harvey, *The Condition of Postmodernity* (London: Blackwell, 1990), 89.

5. Quoted in Graham Ward, *Cities of God*, Radical Orthodoxy (London: Routledge, 2000), 60.

6. Ibid., 59.

7. Terry Johnson, "The Pastor's Public Ministry: Part I," *Westminster Theological Journal* 60 (1998): 140, quoted in D. G. Hart and John R. Muether, *With Reverence and Awe: Returning to the Basics of Reformed Worship* (Phillipsburg, N.J.: P&R Publishing, 2002), 157.

8. For a fascinating discussion of these issues, tinged by feminism, see Thomas Staubli and Silvia Schroer, *Body Symbolism in the Bible*, trans. Linda M. Maloney (Collegeville, Minn.: Liturgical Press, 1998).

9. John Calvin, "The Necessity of Reforming the Church" in *Selected Works of John Calvin: Tracts and Letters*, 7 vols., ed. by Henry Beveridge and Jules Bonnet, trans. Henry Beveridge (Grand Rapids: Baker, [1844] 1983), 1:123–234.

10. For more, see my "The Gospel, Gregory VII, and Modern Theology," in *Modern Theology* (forthcoming).

11. Sacraments, to be sure, are miraculous in a proper sense. That is, they are special acts of God by which He reveals and communicates Himself to us. But what makes the Supper a miraculous meal is not the fact that God works within it to nourish us; He does *that* with every meal. What makes the Supper miraculous is the fact that Christ has ordained this meal to be a means of union and communion with Him.

12. I owe the idea of worship as a series of "postures" to my student, Kate Ramsey.

13. Paul Cartledge, *Spartan Reflections* (Berkeley: University of California Press, 2001), 18.

14. Simon Price, *Religions of the Ancient Greeks*, 25. Much of the information in the following paragraph is drawn from Price's superb summary, 25–46.

15. Ibid., 33–34.

16. Keith Bradley, "The Roman Family at Dinner," in *Meals in a Social Context: Aspects of the Communal Meal in the Hellenistic and Roman World*, ed. by Inge Nielsen and Hanne Sigismund Nielsen (Aarhus: Aarhus UP, 1998), 50.

17. Quoted in L. Michael White, "Regulating Fellowship in the Communal Meal: Early Jewish and Christian Evidence," in ibid., 183.

18. Inge Nielsen, "Royal Banquets: The Development of Royal Banquets and Banqueting Halls from Alexander to the Tetrarchs," in ibid., 124–146.

19. White, "Regulating Fellowship," in ibid., 181–182.

20. For details of the imperial cult in Asia Minor, see Simon Price, *Rituals and Power: The Roman Imperial Cult in Asia Minor* (Cambridge: Cambridge UP, 1984), esp. chapters 5 and 8. For a glimpse of the interconnections of religious ritual and Roman imperial power several centuries later, see the extended description of a festival in Egypt in Ramsay MacMullen, *Corruption and the Decline of Rome* (New Haven: Yale, 1988), 66.

21. Plutarch, *Life of Solon*. See the discussion in Richard Seaford, *Reciprocity and Ritual: Homer and Tragedy in the Developing City-State* (Oxford: Clarendon, 1994), 82, 107.

22. The passage is summarized by Meeks, *Origins of Christian Morality*, 96.

23. Jonathan Brumberg-Kraus, "'Not by Bread Alone. . .': The Ritualization of Food and Table Talk in the Passover *Seder* and in the Last Supper," in *Semeia* 86 ("Food and Drink in the Biblical World"), ed. by Jan Villem van Henten (Atlanta: SBL, 1999), 185–186.

24. Hanne Sigismund Nielsen, "Roman Children at Mealtimes," in Nielsen and Nielsen, eds., *Meals in a Social Context*, 56–66.

NOTES FOR CHAPTER 4

1. Much of the following is inspired by Scott Hafemann's wonderful and richly detailed exegesis in *Paul, Moses, and the History of Israel: The Letter / Spirit Contrast and the Argument from Scripture in 2 Corinthians 3* (Tubingen: Mohr, 1995).

2. Much of the following section is based on John Milbank's deconstruction of Aristotelian virtue in *Theology and Social Theory*, 351–362, and Stanley Hauerwas,

"Only Theology Overcomes Ethics: Or, What 'Ethicists' Must Learn from Jenson," in *A Better Hope: Resources for a Church Confronting Capitalism, Democracy, and Postmodernity* (Grand Rapids: Brazos Press, 2000), 117–128.

3. Quoted in Meeks, *Origins of Christian Morality*, 150.

4. Aristotle's "great-souled" man is as self-absorbed as the gods of paganism. Kristjan Kristjansson has recently argued that Aristotle's notion of *megalopsychos* is central to Aristotle's ethics, and essential to the achievement of happiness. See the review of his book by Peter Goldie, "A Modest Sort of Pridefulness," *Times Literary Supplement* 5176 (June 14, 2002), 11.

5. *Theology and Social Theory*, chapter 11.

6. Stanley Hauerwas, *The Peaceable Kingdom: A Primer in Christian Ethics* (Notre Dame: University of Notre Dame Press, 1983), 108.

7. Ibid., 109–110.

8. *City of God*, 5.12. Throughout this section, I am quoting the translation of Henry Betteson (London: Penguin, 1984).

9. Ibid.

10. Ibid., 5.19. Modern scholars have confirmed Augustine's insight, highlighting the central importance of *philotimia*, the love of honor, in Greco-Roman culture.

11. Ibid., 5.18.

12. It's worthwhile to stop a moment and contemplate the force of that "in consequence."

13. This and the preceding citations are from *City of God*, 19.23–25.

14. Ibid., 5.12.

15. Ramsay Macmullen, *Corruption and the Decline of Rome* (New Haven: Yale, 1988), 69.

16. Meeks, *Origins of Christian Morality*, 42.

17. Wes Howard-Brook, *Church Before Christianity*, 80–81.

18. All of the quotations are derived, sometimes with slight modifications, from statements of Cicero and other Roman writers, which I culled from Carlin A. Barton's lively *Roman Honor: The Fire in the Bones* (Berkeley: University of California Press, 2001).

19. Livy records a fable of Menenius Agrippa, which warns the plebs of Rome against revolt by imagining Rome as a body. In the fable, which is repeated in the first scene of *Coriolanus*, parts of the body refuse to feed the stomach, and the body wastes away as a result (*History of Rome*, 2.32; cited in Sinclair B. Ferguson, *The Holy Spirit*, Contours of Christian Theology [Downers Grove, Ill.: InterVarsity, 1996], 192–193).

20. Hansen in Wallace. Hansen's article is a careful and illuminating discussion of the different meanings of *polis* in Aristotle.

21. These reflections were stimulated by R. Paul Stevens, *The Other Six Days: Vocation, Work, and Ministry in Biblical Perspective* (Grand Rapids: Eerdmans, 1999), esp. 140–145.

22. Rodney Stark, *The Rise of Christianity: How the Obscure, Marginal Jesus Movement Became the Dominant Religious Force in the Western World in a Few Centuries* (San

Francisco: Harper/Collins, 1997), 82.

23. Ibid., 83–84.

24. Dinesh D'Souza, *What's So Great About America*, 189–190.

25. "The Impossible Culture: Wilde as Modern Prophet," in Rieff, *The Feeling Intellect: Selected Essays* (Chicago: University of Chicago Press, 1990), 273–290.

26. Ibid., 279.

27. See Marcus Borg, *Conflict, Holiness, and Politics in the Teachings of Jesus* (Harrisburg: Trinity Press International, [1984] 1998).

28. "Impossible Culture," 279.

29. Ibid., 278.

30. Robert Jenson, *The Works of God*, vol. 2 of *Systematic Theology* (Oxford: Oxford UP, 1999), 87.

31. For an honest assessment, see Mary Eberstadt, "The Elephant in the Sacristry," *The Weekly Standard* 7 (June 17, 2002), 22–33.

32. Paul Shaughnessy, "Are the Jesuits Catholic?" *The Weekly Standard* 7 (June 3, 2002), 27–31. Shaughnessy's shocking article is a review of Peter McDonough and Eugene C. Bianchi's book, *Passionate Uncertainty: Inside the American Jesuits* (University of California Press).

33. This is related to what Alasdair MacIntyre has called the "emotivism" that characterizes contemporary moral discussion. Emotivism is "the doctrine that all evaluative judgments and more specifically all moral judgments are *nothing but* expressions of preference, expressions of attitude or feeling" (*After Virtue: A Study in Moral Theory*, 2nd ed. [Notre Dame, Ind.: University of Notre Dame Press, (1981) 1984], 11–12).

34. Chrysostom recounts the story of his ordination in *On the Priesthood*, Book 1. Both Augustine's reluctance to be ordained bishop and the custom of the Coptic church are mentioned in Philip Schaff, ed., *Nicene and Post-Nicene Fathers* (Grand Rapids: Eerdmans, [1889] 1983), 9:35, note 2. On Gregory the Great, see Bertram Colgrave, ed., *The Earliest Life of Gregory the Great, by an Anonymous Monk of Whitby* (Cambridge: Cambridge UP, 1985), 85–87.

35. See Thomas C. Oden, *Ministry Through Word and Sacrament*, vol. 2 of *Classical Pastoral Care* (New York: Crossroad, 1989), 13–17.

36. *No Place for Truth*, chapter 6.

37. Ephraim Radner, *The End of the Church: A Pneumatology of Christian Division in the West* (Grand Rapids: Eerdmans, 1998).

NOTES FOR CHAPTER 5

1. T. S. Eliot's claim that the West remains Christian so long as it has not definitively become something else was perhaps adequate when he wrote it. But he wrote a long time ago.

2. Hauerwas, *After Christendom?* (Nashville: Abingdon, 1991), 166, note 8. In this same endnote, Hauerwas moves in a somewhat different direction, claiming that "I do not seek to make a virtue out of minority status per se. Being out of power or oppressed can be an occasion for corruption as much as being in power. . .

. . the question for Christians is not whether we rule, but how. Our difficulty has been the confusion that the rule of Christ must take the form of domination promised by Caesar."

3. Rodney Clapp, *A Peculiar People: The Church as Culture in a Post-Christian Society* (Downers Grove, Ill.: IVP, 1996), 30.

4. Rodney Stark, *Rise of Christianity*, 156–157.

5. Ibid., 160–161.

6. Ibid.

7. George Steiner, *In Bluebeard's Castle: Notes Towards the Redefinition of Culture* (New Haven: Yale, 1971), 107.

8. *A Peculiar People*, 29–30, 39.

9. Oliver O'Donovan, *Desire of Nations*, 216.

10. Ibid., 194.

11. Ibid., 195.

12. The following paragraphs summarize Yoder's discussion in "The Constantinian Sources of Western Social Ethics," chap. 7 of *The Priestly Kingdom: Social Ethics as Gospel* (Notre Dame: University of Notre Dame Press, 1984).

13. Ibid., 146–147.

14. Ibid., 145.

15. *Desire of Nations*, 222.

16. Ibid., 223.

17. Ibid., 223–224.

18. Dieter Georgi, *Theocracy*, 57.

19. This line of interpretation is taken from James B. Jordan, *A Brief Reader's Guide to Revelation* (Niceville, Fla.: Transfiguration Press, 1999).